CAMBRIDGE LIBRARY COLLECTION

Books of enduring scholarly value

History

The books reissued in this series include accounts of historical events and movements by eye-witnesses and contemporaries, as well as landmark studies that assembled significant source materials or developed new historiographical methods. The series includes work in social, political and military history on a wide range of periods and regions, giving modern scholars ready access to influential publications of the past.

An Account of a Voyage to Establish a Colony at Port Philip

James Tuckey (1776–1816) was a naval officer who was appointed first lieutenant on H.M.S. *Calcutta*. In 1802 the ship was given orders to sail to New South Wales, Australia, to survey the harbour at Port Phillip (now in the state of Victoria) and to establish a colony. The *Calcutta* departed from Portsmouth in April 1803 and arrived in New South Wales in October. After Tuckey returned from the assignment, he published this account in 1805. He begins the work by explaining the motives behind establishing the colony – it was to be used for convicts, some of whom he was transporting on the ship. The first four chapters discuss the journey but the final chapter focuses on the attempts to establish a colony and encounters with the indigenous population, and gives a survey of the coastline. Port Phillip became the city of Melbourne, and this work is a valuable source about its early years of settlement.

Cambridge University Press has long been a pioneer in the reissuing of out-of-print titles from its own backlist, producing digital reprints of books that are still sought after by scholars and students but could not be reprinted economically using traditional technology. The Cambridge Library Collection extends this activity to a wider range of books which are still of importance to researchers and professionals, either for the source material they contain, or as landmarks in the history of their academic discipline.

Drawing from the world-renowned collections in the Cambridge University Library, and guided by the advice of experts in each subject area, Cambridge University Press is using state-of-the-art scanning machines in its own Printing House to capture the content of each book selected for inclusion. The files are processed to give a consistently clear, crisp image, and the books finished to the high quality standard for which the Press is recognised around the world. The latest print-on-demand technology ensures that the books will remain available indefinitely, and that orders for single or multiple copies can quickly be supplied.

The Cambridge Library Collection will bring back to life books of enduring scholarly value (including out-of-copyright works originally issued by other publishers) across a wide range of disciplines in the humanities and social sciences and in science and technology.

An Account of a Voyage to Establish a Colony at Port Philip

in His Majesty's Ship Calcutta,
in the Years 1802-3-4

JAMES HINGSTON TUCKEY

CAMBRIDGE
UNIVERSITY PRESS

CAMBRIDGE UNIVERSITY PRESS

Cambridge, New York, Melbourne, Madrid, Cape Town,
Singapore, São Paolo, Delhi, Tokyo, Mexico City

Published in the United States of America by Cambridge University Press, New York

www.cambridge.org
Information on this title: www.cambridge.org/9781108039031

© in this compilation Cambridge University Press 2011

This edition first published 1805
This digitally printed version 2011

ISBN 978-1-108-03903-1 Paperback

A

VOYAGE

TO ESTABLISH A COLONY AT

PORT PHILIP IN BASS's STRAIT.

&c. &c.

A

Strahan and Prefton, Printers,
New-Street Square, London.

AN

ACCOUNT

OF A

VOYAGE

TO ESTABLISH A COLONY AT

PORT PHILIP IN BASS's STRAIT,

ON THE SOUTH COAST OF

NEW SOUTH WALES,

IN HIS MAJESTY's SHIP CALCUTTA,

IN THE YEARS 1802-3-4.

By J. H. TUCKEY, Esq.

FIRST LIEUTENANT OF THE CALCUTTA.

" Bear Britain's thunder, and her cross display,
" To the bright regions of the rising day ;
" Tempt icy seas, where scarce the waters roll,
" Where clearer flames glow round the frozen pole,
" Or under southern skies, exalt their sails,
" Led by new stars, and borne by spicy gales."

POPE'S WINDSOR FOREST.

LONDON:

PRINTED FOR LONGMAN, HURST, REES, AND ORME,
PATERNOSTER-ROW ;
AND J. C. MOTTLEY, PORTSMOUTH.

1805.

TO

Sir F. I. HARTWELL, Kt.

ONE OF THE HONOURABLE THE COMMISSIONERS
OF HIS MAJESTY'S NAVY.

DEAR SIR,

IN dedicating the following Narrative to you, I am aware that I shall be suspected of a great share of personal vanity; and, perhaps, in this instance, not of more than I really possess: for to be honoured with

A 3   your

your friendship may well be a source
of pride to the most humble.

To you, Sir, I feel it necessary
to account for the barrenness of pro-
fessional information, which may be
remarked in this Narrative. The Calcutta's voyage, though comprising
the circumnavigation of the globe,
was never intended to be a voyage
of discovery; and from the undeviating route which she pursued, it was
particularly barren of events which
could lead to scientific observations :
indeed, this track has, of late years,
been

been so often traversed by the ablest navigators and men of science, that the most attentive diligence can scarcely glean any thing that has not already been the subject of investigation. In appearing before the Public under these disadvantages, I am at least certain of deriving one very high gratification, that of gratefully acknowledging the continued kindness I have received from you, Sir, since I first launched upon the world's wide waves; and should it ever be my good fortune to be engaged in any future project of dis-

A 4 covery,

covery, I trust I shall, at least, have a just claim to diligence and perseverance.

I have the honour to be,

DEAR SIR,

Your faithful and

obliged humble Servant,

J. H. TUCKEY.

PORTSMOUTH,
OCT. 29, 1804,

PREFACE.

THE Author presumes to claim the indulgence of the Public towards the literary faults, which he fears are too numerous in the following pages. He trusts it will be recollected that a sailor's life affords few moments of " learned ease;" and that he is fitted, both by education and habit, more for action than for thought. Connected arrangement, and logical deductions, are the offspring of retired meditation; but meditation, pensive Nymph, " shuns the noise of folly," or flies before the mirth of thoughtlessness : hence it will scarcely be expected to find a correct work produced amidst the interruptions of active service,

service, or the continual calls of *subordi-nate* duty.

With respect to information, the author hopes some will be found new, and the whole not entirely uninteresting. Some part of it is necessarily derived from the information of others; and for its cor-rectness the Author can only state his own belief, as being received from per-sons capable of judging, and who could have no interest in misrepresentation. For the paucity of nautical observations, he conceives no apology is necessary. On this head he has confined himself to a few notes upon points which he con-sidered most interesting to navigation. A minute detail of winds, weather, and all the common occurrences of a ship at sea, he suspects would neither

8   amuse

amuse nor instruct the majority of his readers; and to those who find entertainment in " ditto weather, employed occasionally," he recommends the logbook publications of some recent navigators.

CON-

CONTENTS.

CHAP. I.

MOTIVES which induced Government to employ King's ships in transporting Convicts to New South Wales.—Intention of establishing a Colony in Bass's Strait.—Calcutta appointed to convey thither the first establishment.—Passage from England to Teneriffe, and the Cape Verd Islands. - - - Page 1

CHAP. II.

From the Cape Verd Islands to Rio de Janeiro.—North Atlantic Ocean.—St. Sebastian.—Population.—Manners, Climate, and Disseases. 31

CHAP. III.

Rio de Janeiro.—Productions, Trade.—Slaves, Indians.—Police and Courts of Justice.—State of Defence.—Political Situation. - - 77

CHAP. IV.

From Rio de Janeiro to the Cape of Good Hope.—Islands of Tristan d'Acunha.—Cape Town.—Simmon's Town.—Dutch.—Departure from the Cape.—Island of St. Paul.—Arrival at Port Philip. - - - - *Page* 115

CHAP. V.

Transactions at Port Philip from the Arrival to the Sailing of the Calcutta.—Survey of the Port.—Natives.—Communication with Port Jackson.—Determination to remove the Colony.—Examination of Western Port. - - - 153

ADDENDA.

Nº   Page
  I.   -   -   -   -   -   -   215

 II. List of Plants found at Port Philip, Oc-
       tober, November, and December,
       1803.   -   -   -   218

III. Meteorological Journal for the Months
       of October, November, and Decem-
       ber, at Port Philip.   -   -   220

 IV. Observations on the various kinds of
       Timber found in New South Wales. 224

  V. Observations respecting the selection of
       Convicts for transportation, and on
       the means of preserving health on the
       voyage.   -   -   -   -   231

ERRATA.

Page 5, *line* 9, *Note,* *for* Hinders *read* Flinders.
62, *line* 3, *for* gate *read* grate.

A

VOYAGE

TO

NEW SOUTH WALES.

CHAP. I.

Motives which induced Government to employ King's ships in transporting Convicts to New South Wales.—Intention of establishing a Colony in Bass's Strait.—Calcutta appointed to convey thither the first establishment.—Passage from England to Teneriffe, and the Cape Verd Islands.

THE motives, which, in the year 1802, induced Government to employ King's ships in transporting convicts to New South Wales, appear to have had their foundation, not only in principles of

B   eco-

economy, but also in the union of many other advantages, which promised to be the result. Until this period, merchant ships had always been chartered to convey there victims of vice and folly to the place of their destination : independent of the expence of these vessels, which was a dead loss to Government, the abuses disgraceful to humanity, that too frequently took place on board of them, called aloud for correction. By employing king's ships on this service, a number of officers and seamen would be provided for, who might otherwise emigrate to foreign services, and be totally lost to their country ; and again, it must naturally be supposed, that the Officers, having neither pecuniary nor commercial intereſt in the voyage, would conduct

duct it upon principles very different from those of mercenary, and perhaps illiterate traders ; at the same time that the former would be enabled to keep the convicts in a better state of discipline, and also be more careful of their health, by that constant attention to cleanliness, which characterizes the British navy. To these obvious and immediate advantages, was added another, which, though merely speculative, promised, if successful, to exceed them all. It was known, that timber, supposed to be peculiarly adapted to naval uses, might be procured at New South Wales with little difficulty or expence, and in the present time of its encreasing scarcity and great demand at home, both for public and private service, this was an object of the first

B 2   national

(4)

national importance * : it was therefore determined to try the experiment, when, by the conclusion of peace, the nation began to breathe, after the late long and arduous contest. The ships of the navy best calculated for this purpose, were decidedly those built for the East India Company, and purchased into the King's service during the war; and accordingly, the Glatton sailed for Port-Jackson in September, with 330 male, and 170 female convicts.

The Calcutta, another ship of the like class, was intended to pursue the same route, and was commissioned in

* See the Letters between the Court of Directors of the East India Company, and the Commissioners for the Affairs of India.

ASIATIC REGISTER, July 1801

4   Octo-

October following * ; but while fitting out, a material change was made in her destination. Since the discovery of Bass's Strait †, it had entered into the contemplation of Government to esta‑ blish a settlement at its western en‑ trance, as well from commercial, as political motives. In the first respect, it would give the greatest encouragement to the speculations carried on for seals,

---

* The Glatton and Calcutta were fitted exactly alike. They were armed *en flute,* having only 18 guns on the upper deck ; rigged as 56 gun ships, with a compliment of 170 men.

† Bass's Strait feparates New Holland from Van Diemen's Land, in lat. 39° S. ; it was discovered by Mr. Bass, surgeon of his Majesty's ship Reliance, in an open whale boat, in the year 1799. It was afterwards surveyed by Mr. Bass and Mr. Hinders, fecond lieutenant of the Reliance, and found to be from 100 to 130 miles in breadth, affording a clear passage from the South Sea into the Indian Ocean.

B 3 and

and sea-elephants, to the islands in the
Straits, to have a secure port in their
vicinity, where the produce might be
collected until ready for exportation :
in the next place, this measure would
prevent any rival nations from establishing themselves on this coast, who might
become troublesome neighbours to our
colony at Port Jackson, which must no
longer be considerad as a contemptible
part of the British dominions ; and to
which, the possession of Bass's Strait
would give us a less tedious and circui-
tous access.   Port Philip *, on the
north shore of the Straits, which was

---

* Port Philip was difcovered by Acting Lieutenant
John Murray, in his Majefty's armed brig Lady Nel-
son, and by him named Port King ; which was after-
wards changed by Governor King to Port Philip, after
Captain Arthur Philip, the firft Governor of New
South Wales.

reported

reported to be an excellent harbour, seemed, from its geographical position, to possess all the advantages required in the proposed settlement. To carry this project into execution, several necessary alterations took place in the equipment of the Calcutta; and the command of her was conferred on Captain Daniel Woodriff, an experienced naval officer, who had before visited New South Wales, as Agent of Transports. As the Calcutta was found insufficient to convey the necessary stores for the new settlement, the Ocean, a merchant-ship of 500 tons burthen, was chartered for that purpose, and was afterwards to proceed to China, for a cargo of teas: on board her were embarked the civil, and part of the military officers, and settlers; together with

B 4   the

the greater part of the stores, provisions, and implements of agriculture; while the Calcutta conveyed a detachment of marines, the whole of the convicts, their wives and children, and the remainder of the stores, as well as a considerable quantity for Port Jackson *.

The

* The following was the Establishment for the New Colony.

Civil.

1 Lieutenant Governor, - 480*l. per ann.*
1 Deputy Judge-advocate *, - 10*s. per diem.*
1 Chaplain, - - 10*s.*
1 Deputy Commissary, - 7*s.* 6*d.*
1 Surgeon, - - 10*s.*
2 Assistant Surgeons; 1st, 7*s.* 6*d.*—2d, 5*s.*
1 Surveyor, - - 7*s.* 6*d.*
1 Mineralogist, - - 7*s.* 6*d.*
2 Superintendants of Convicts, each 50*l. per ann.*
4 Overseers, each, - 25*l.*
1 Superintendant of Artificers, - 45*l.*

* This Officer remained in England.

Military

The Calcutta arrived at Portsmouth, from the river Medway, in the middle of February 1803, where she waited the junction of the Ocean, which was protracted until the 8th of April. The first weeks of this month the winds had been constantly from the eastward; but various trifling causes, which commonly retard expeditions of this nature, prevented our taking advantage of them, and when these obstacles were removed,

---

Military (Marines).

- 1 Captain Commandant. (Lieut. Governor.)
- 2 1st Lieutenants.
- 1 2d ditto.
- 3 Serjeants.
- 3 Corporals.
- 2 Drums.
- 39 Rank and File.
- 5 Women, and 1 child.
- 307 Male Convicts, with 17 of their wives; and 7 children.

the

the winds, as if determined to shew
their contempt for the ambitious, and
too often short-sighted views of man,
suddenly changed to the westward, and
blew with a degree of violence that left
no hopes of succeeding, should we attempt to beat down Channel. Perhaps
no fituation can be more irksome than
this to a sailor; when his mind is made
up for departure, every delay that im-
pedes it, is felt as a misfortune; and
yet such is the contradiction in the
mind of man, that while he wishes, he
fears the removal of these impediments,
and would still linger out another day,
to accomplish something which is yet
undone, or perhaps to take *another* last
farewell of friends, to whom he has already bidden fifty times adieu. The
first moment of a favourable wind we
took

took advantage of, and quitted St. Helens on the morning of the 26th; but on the evening of the next day, the wind again veering to the weftward, and blowing hard, obliged us to run through the Needles, and take shelter in Yarmouth Roads. The following morning, with a strong breeze from the northward, we again put to sea, and cleared the Channel on the 29th. This part of a foreign voyage, though a mere point as to distance, is reckoned by sailors the most material and difficult; for the Englifh Channel is so situated, that the prevailing westerly winds make the egress from it extremely precarious, particularly in winter.

In bidding farewel to England, it may naturally be supposed, that the feelings of our motley crew would be as
various

various as their situations, their prospects, or their characters; yet the general sentiment seemed to be that of
entire indifference : a few women alone,
whose birth and education had promised
them a far different fate, were affected
by this heart-rending, though voluntary,
exile from their native country; and

> " Shudd'ring still, to face the distant deep,
> " Return'd, and wept, and still return'd to weep."

Among the convicts on board, were
some who, by prodigality, and its attendant vices, had degraded themselves
from a respectable rank in society, and
were indebted to the lenity of their pro-
secutors alone for an escape from the
last sentence of the law. Some of these
men were accompanied by their wives,
who had married them in the sunshine
of prosperity, when the world smiled
deceit-

deceitfully, and their path of life appeared strewed with unfading flowers; in the season of adversity, they would not be separated, but reposed their heads upon the same thorny pillow; and as they had shared with them the cup of joy, they refused not that of sorrow. Those alone who know the miserable and degraded situation of a transported felon, can appretiate the degree of connubial love, that could induce these women to accompany their guilty husbands in their exile. The laws can only make distinction in crimes, while the criminals, whatever may have been their former situation in life, must suffer alike for crimes of the same nature: it therefore entirely depended on us to ameliorate their condition, and grant such indulgences, as the nature and degree of
the

the crime, and the otherwise general character and conduct of the prisoner seemed to deserve. To these helpless females, all the attentions that humanity dictated, and that the nature of our service would admit, were extended, but still it was impossible to separate their situations entirely from their guilty husbands, they were consequently far, very far, from being comfortable; and one of them, borne down by the first hardships of the voyage, which she felt with redoubled force from being far advanced in her preguancy, fell a victim to her misplaced affection before our arrival at Teneriffe.

The ships anchored before Santa Cruz on the 17th of May, and having completed their water, and procured a supply

ply

ply of wine, sailed again on the 21st.
While laying at Santa Cruz, fresh beef
was served throughout the ship, and
as a slight indication of scurvy was observed in some of the prisoners, a large
quantity of vegetables and lemons was
laid in for sea-store. The free use of
fresh water was also permitted to wash
the convict's clothes; an indulgence,
the beneficial effects of which cannot
be too highly valued. In voyages of
this nature, where a great number of
people are crowded together, to whom
it is not always possible to permit such
exercise as is necessary to health,
cleanliness is the only preventative of
disease; and, independent of any other
necessity, it will always be eligible to
put into any convenient port for that
purpose alone.

It

It would appear, that the island of Teneriffe deserves the high character it has received for salubrity of climate. We attended the funeral of a native, who had lived 26 years beyond the common life of man, " after which all is but labour and trouble." His brother, who attended the funeral, was 94, and seemed to put his own mortal deftiny at a distance.

The thermometer stood between 70 and 72, a temperature, perhaps, more congenial to human life, than any other.

The celebrated Peak has by no means the grand appearance that the traveller is taught to expect, but its apparent altitude is much diminished, by the general height of the circumjacent mountains ;

tains : indeed, the appearance of the
eastern side of the island gives a very
unfavourable impression of its value ; a
confused assemblage of rocky hills,
heaped upon, and crossing each other
in every direction, present themselves
to the eye, like the waves of the ocean
disturbed by the fury of contending
winds and currents. These precipices
are bare of vegetation, except where a
ftarved brufh-wood insinuates its roots
between the rugged masses of volcanic
matter, or in a few spots where the industry of man has conquered the steri-
lity of nature, and raised a scanty crop
of barley or maize : as we recede from
the sea-coast, however, the country im-
proves, and affords many prospects of
romantic grandeur, and luxuriant ferti-
lity. The town of Santa Cruz is built with

C   tole-

tolerable regularity, on a gentle accli-
vity, on the west side of the Bay: the
landing-place is defended from the sea,
by a projecting rocky point, and a good
ftone pier. Being merely a King's port,
it derives but little advantage from commerce, which is entirely carried on from
the port of Orotava, on the west side of
the island. Teneriffe has no manufactures of any consequence, except its
wine, nor does it produce corn enough
for its own consumption; for this, and
also for poultry, it depends upon the
other islands, particularly the Grand
Canary, with which there is a constant
intercourse by boats. The importation
of foreign linen, or cotton manufactures,
is prohibited, and consequently those of
the English looms bear a high price, and
are universally worn; which proves, that

great

great restraints laid on any articles of merchandize, serve but to enhance their value, to make them be sought after with more avidity, and to encourage their clandestine importation. It was found, that the friars and women, whose persons were held free from scrutiny, smuggled on shore great quantities of these goods; and in consequence, neither are now permitted to go on board any vessel, without express leave from the Governor. The importation of tobacco, by private traders, is also forbidden, Government drawing part of its colonial revenue from the exclusive sale of this article.

Santa Cruz has but three churches; rather a small number for the religion of its inhabitants, which teaches, that

to

to " give to the church, is to lend un-
to God ;" and that, being buried in the
sacred vestments of a religious order,
ensures a favourable reception from St.
Peter, who more readily opens to them
the portal of everlasting life. In vifit-
ing places of public worship in Roman
Catholic countries, we cease to wonder
at the deeply imprinted superstition of
the people; children, before they can
scarce speak, are taught to set a sacred
value on the ridiculous grimace of de-
votion, and a father brings his boy, not
three years old, to lisp his *ave maria*,
and count his little rosary before the
altar. This early impression it is impossible can ever be erased ; imitation, at
laft, becomes a second nature ; in ma-
turer years, reason, in vain, attempts to
pull down the firm bulwark of superstition,

stition, and narrow-minded bigotry becomes the characteristic of the man.
Toleration of religious opinions has not
yet reached this island, and, whatever
may be his real persuasion, every person
residing here must conform to the external ceremonies of the established
church: a heretic is still denied the
boon of a consecrated grave, and his
hapless ghost must be contented with a
mansion in the unpurified bosom of his
mother earth, unless it prefers a more
extensive sepulchre in the ocean. The
bodies of those who die in the faith, are
usually interred in the churches; the
coffins have no cover, and are filled up
with quick-lime, which decomposing the
flesh, the bones are afterwards removed
to a general charnel-house. This example deserves to be universally followed,

C 3   but

but the prejudices of education, which teaches us to consider disturbing the dead as a species of horrid sacrilege *, still wars against our better judgment, and perpetuates the noisome and acknowledged evil of crowded churchyards.

It appears to be a custom of ancient origin throughout Europe, (perhaps antecedent to heraldic achievements,) to

---

* The veneration paid to the mortal remains of our ancestors is generally dignified with the appellation of natural affection; it however may more properly be deduced from pride of birth, united with religious superstition. In Europe, it appears to be almost the last spark from the dying embers of feudal government. In China, where every beggar can trace his pedigree to one of the three hundred families, the dead are objects of more care than the living; feasts are held in honour of them, and their graves are continually adorned with silken streamers, and strewed with fresh flowers.

denote

denote the death of any member of the family, by some symbol affixed to the house of the deceased; at Teneriffe, a branch of the palm-tree is placed over the door or window for this purpose.

The manners of the inhabitants in general are those of the mother-country; a few families, of which the Lieutenant Governor's is the chief, adopt the French customs in dress and society; and the vivacity and liberal manners of the latter, afford a striking contrast to the austere gravity, and prudish reserve, of the former. The return of peace has not yet brought back to the iſland the English, who were driven from it by the war; and the necessary business of any British vessels that touch here, is at present transacted by Mr. Armstrong, a native of the iſland.

C 4   In

In its present state, Santa Cruz could scarce make a successful defence against a well-conducted *coup de main*; the fortifications are in ruins, and the garrison consists of a miserable rabble, who, to appearance, would verify the old adage about running away. The pier is, however, defended by a battery, which might annoy the invaders, and which ought, therefore, to be immediately silenced; for this purpose, one line of battle fhip would be fully sufficient. A shot from this battery pursued its too unerring course, and deprived the Navy of the brave Bowen, at the same time that it took off the arm of Nelson. In the church of Neustra Senora de Constantia, is suspended the union flag, left behind by Nelson in his unsuccessful attack on the island in 1799. It was pointed

out

out to us with every mark of national pride by our conductor, who, after a long harangue on the courage of their troops, was drily requested by an English Officer to be particularly careful of this trophy of their prowess, for that Nelson might probably one day return, and call for it.

The water here has a soft, soapy taste, and I believe a slight purgative quality; it is conducted from the mountains to a stone fountain, which throws up three *jets d'eau.* The island produces a species of pine-tree, which is used in the construction of the houses, and in small vessels; we were here too early for the fruits of the island, which are those peculiar to the tropics. Vegetables were plenty, onions in particu-

lar

lar are remarkably good ; and as they
are not to be procured at Rio de Janeiro, it is advisable to lay in a large
stock of them here : fowls cost about
half a crown each : sheep are scarce,
and bad ; and hogs neither cheap nor
good *. The only fish we saw, were
large mackarel, vast shoals of which
come into the bay at this season ; they
are caught with hook and line, and attracted towards the boats by fires of
the dried pine, which give a bright blaze,
and of a serene evening the bay presents the appearance of a magnificent
marine illumination.

Between England and Teneriffe we
lost four convicts by death ; two of these

* Beef is about 4d. per pound. The price of Teneriffe wine has increased within a few years ; the beſt
is now 20l. a pipe, and that of inferior quality 16l.

had

had been embarked in the last stages
of consumption, vainly hoping that a
warmer climate might restore their
healths.

From Teneriffe, we pursued our course
towards the Cape Verd Islands, and on
the 25th of May made the isle of Sal,
along which we coasted at the distance
of six or seven miles, without seeing any
thing that could induce a stranger to land
on it from choice ; not a trace of cultivation, nor of inhabitants, was to be seen ;
nor did a single shrub enliven the dreary
brown of the parched soil. This island
has but few stationary inhabitants, but
is frequented for the salt which is collected on it, with which it supplies America, and the West Indies.

On

On the morning of the 26th, we stood
close in for St. Jago, the largest of the
Cape Verd Islands, and ranged along its
S. E. fide at from one to two miles distance. This side of the island is broken,
and uneven, in some places bound
by projecting shelves of rock, the lower parts being excavated by the continual action of the water; in other spots
are small sandy coves, defended by reefs
on which the sea beats with violence.
This island affords an agreeable prospect to the distressed mariner ; the sides
of the more gently ascending hills
are covered with a verdant carpet,
upon which numerous herds of cattle
are seen grazing, and in the vallies are
groves of cocoa-nuts and bannanas surrounding the habitations of the natives.
The harbour of Praya, laying on the south
side

side of the island, is, during the regular N. E. trade-wind, perfectly secure, but it is exposed to the tornadoes, which in the months of August and September often blow from the southward. The natives appeared desirous of our landing, by waving their handkerchiefs on the rock as we passed along : hoping some of them might be induced to come on board with fruit, we stood close into the bay, but not a canoe was to be seen, and it was not an object of sufficient consequence, to suffer any delay by sending a boat on shore. The town, from which we were distant about five miles, is the seat of government; to appearance it consists of a few wretched clay huts adjoining the fort, which alone is white-washed. A lucrative trade is carried on from this island to America and the

the West Indies in mules : by breeding these animals, and by supplying ships with refreshments, the inhabitants support themselves. The mother-country feels so little the importance of these islands, that scarce any precautions are taken for their defence : a Creole is often governor-general; and the inferior islands are sometimes governed by Mulattoes.

A thick haze always obscures these islands, and prevents their being seen at the distance that might be expected from their altitudes : this, I suppose, proceeds from the exhalations arising from the Salt lakes, and this haze is much thicker and more opake when the sun is in the Northern tropic.

CHAP.

CHAP. II.

From the Cape Verd Islands to Rio de Janeiro.—North Atlantic Ocean.—St. Sebastian.—Population.—Manners, Climate, and Diseases.

June. FROM the Cape Verd Islands to the vicinity of the line, the N.E. trade-wind continued to impel us forward with undeviating celerity. In this space, it is impossible not to mark, with emotions of pleasure, the beautiful atmospherical pictures which the evenings afford: in the direction of the setting sun, the Heavens are seen glowing with orange and purple, blended into the greatest variety of tints, and melting impercep-

2   tibly

tibly into the pure ether of light ceru-
lean blue; in which, the first stars of
evening shine with the most brilliant
silvery lustre; but,

>   ———Who can paint
> Like Nature? Can Imagination boast,
> Amidst its gay creation, hues like her's :
> Or, can it mix them with that matchless skill,
> And lose them in each other ?

This beautiful appearance of the
Heavens is confined to the Northern
Tropic : in the Southern, the air is
commonly loaded with gloomy and dense
vapours, that, descending to the horizon, constitute that kind of atmosphere
to which is given the epithet, *hazy*.

The Northern tropical seas are the
peculiar residence of the Dolphin, the
Bonetta, the Albacore, the Skip-jack,
and

and the Flying-fish; the latter is often
seen winging its transient flight, to e-
scape the swift pursuit of the dolphin,
while the voracious shark waits its de-
scent; when, exhausted by the want of
moisture, its wings refuse to bear it
aloft, and it falls helpless into his de-
vouring jaws. The shark is the heredi-
tary foe of sailors; and the moment
one is spied, the whole crew are in-
stantly in arms; often, the day's
allowance of meat is sacrificed to bait
the hook intended to entrap their hungry adversary; while grains, harpoons,
and every missive weapon, are pointed
at his devoted head. When success
attends their operations, and the de-
luded victim is dragged on board, no
pack of hungry fox-hounds can be
more restless, till they receive the re-

D　　　　ward

ward of their labours, than the sailors to
tear out the bowels, and examine the
stomach of the shark. Here they often
recover the pieces of meat used to bait
the hooks, which his sagacity had ex-
tricated; and after cutting off his fins *,
saving his jaws as objects of curiosity,
and reserving a few slices from the tail
to eat, the carcase is again committed
to the watery element.

The peculiar property of tropical at-
mospheres in corroding iron, is well
known: it is almost impossible to keep
any article of that metal from rusting,
even for an hour, without the applica-

* The silvery fibres of sharks' fins are manufactured
into artificial flying-fish, for catching dolphins, &c.
These fins also form a considerable article of trade
between India and China ; the Chinese putting them
into their soups.

tion

tion of oil. The copious vapours exhaled from the earth and sea, in tropical climates, may produce this effect, which is found to decrease as we recede from the equator, either north or south.

In latitude 6° North, we lost the N. E. trade-wind, and for a few days experienced the usual equinoctial calms, and squalls, with heavy rains, and strong easterly currents. The line was crossed in the longitude of 25° W. *, with the usual

---

* Navigators differ in their opinions respecting the most eligible meridian to cross the line on; but agree, that it ought to be between the longitudes of 20° and 25° W.; but by crossing it so far to the eastward as 20°, calms of long continuance, and strong easterly currents, setting into the gulph of Guinea, will commonly be met with; by crossing it to the westward of 25°, strong westerly currents are found setting into the immense bight between Cape St. Au-

gustine

usual visit from Mr. Neptune, his wife, and child. This ceremony, though ridicu-

---

gustine and Florida; the meridian of 23° W. on the line, seems to be the boundary of these different currents. In the various opinions upon this subject, sufficient regard has not been paid to the season of the year. When the sun is far in the northern tropic, the winds to the southward of the line, incline more southerly, and, during the contrary season, they incline more northerly than the regular course of the trade-wind. Intending to touch at Rio Janeiro, between the months of March and September, I would prefer crossing the line in 26 ° W.; and between September and March again in 28°. But if it is not intended to touch at Rio, I would, during the first season, cross the line in 23°; and during the latter, in 25° : crossing the line from the southward, I look upon 27° to be the best meridian, as being not only less liable to calms, but also for the probability of meeting the trade well to the eastward, and perhaps, even to the southward of east. When the sun is in the northern tropic, I would recommend keeping on the last meridian till to the northward of the Cape Verd Isles; for, by coming nearer to these islands at this season, you will most probably meet with calms, and baffling winds.

lous

lous enough, is, when ably executed,
sufficiently amusing: the ugliest persons in the ship are chosen to represent
Neptune, and Amphitrite (but the latter
name being rather too hard of pro-
nunciation, is always familiarized into
Mrs. Neptune); their faces are painted
in the most ridiculous manner, and their
heads are furnished with swabs well
greased and powdered: Neptune's beard
is of the same materials; while a pair of
grains, or a boat-hook, serves him for a
trident: a triumphal car is constructed
with chairs fixed on a gun-carriage, or
wheel-barrow, in which they are seated,
and drawn from the forecastle to the
quarter-deck, by a number of sailors
representing Tritons. After enquiries respecting the ship's destination, saluting
their old acquaintances, and making

D 3   the

the Captain some ridiculous present,
such as a dog or cat, under the name
of a Canary-bird, they are again rolled
forward, and the ceremony of shaving
and ducking their new visitors commences. A large tub of salt water is
prepared, with a stick across it, on which
the visitor is seated ; Neptune's barber,
after lathering his face well, with a mix-
ture of tar and grease, performs the
operation of shaving with a piece of
rusty iron hoop, and when clean scraped,
which is not accomplished without many
wry faces, he is pushed backwards into
the tub, and kept there until complete-
ly soaked.

The vicissitudes of the weather on the
line are greater than any where else on
the surface of the globe. In a moment,
from

from an atmosphere glowing with the fierce rays of a vertical sun, the storm is seen brooding in the horizon, which soon becomes of a pitchy blackness; the dark volume silently and slowly approaches; not a breath ruffles the glassy surface of the main, until, in an instant, it bursts in all the fury of elemental strife. Thomson has so happily painted these equatorial squalls, that I cannot help transcribing the passage :

——In blazing height of noon,
The sun, oppress'd, is plung'd in thickest gloom.
Still Horror reigns, a dreary twilight round,
Of struggling night and day malignant mix'd.
For to the hot equator crouding fast,
Where highly rarefy'd, the yielding air
Admits their stream, incessant vapours roll,
Amazing clouds on clouds continual heap'd;
Or whirl'd impetuous by the gusty wind,
Or silent borne along, heavy and slow,
With the big stores of steaming ocean charg'd.

D 4   Mean-

Meantime, amid these upper seas condens'd

*   *   *   *   *

And by conflicting winds together dash'd,
The Thunder holds her black tremendous throne :
From cloud to cloud the rending Lightnings rage ;
Till, in the furious elemental war
Dissolv'd, the whole precipitated mass
Unbroken floods, and solid torrents pours.

These squalls are, however, short as
they are violent, and the sun soon
bursts forth again in all his former
fervour. The S. E. trade met us two
degrees to the northward of the line, and
accompanied us to 20° South, where it
was succeeded by winds blowing from
every point of the compass *. Our ar-

---

* It is a general principle in the theory of winds,
that the S. E. trade is found to blow in all the southern seas, between the latitudes of 5° and 25° S. This
is, however, subject to very great irregularities in the
South Atlantic Ocean, within 200 leagues of the
American coast, which doubtless proceed from the
great elevation of this continent.

rival

rival at Rio de Janeiro was greatly re-
tarded by the Ocean, whose rate of
sailing was much inferior to the Calcutta's. We reached that Port the last
day of June, and immediately commenced the necessary refittal of the
ship, to enable her to encounter the
long succession of stormy weather,
which the season of the year taught us
to expect in the remainder of our passage to New Holland. The small
Island of Enchardos, about two miles
from the town, was hired with permission of the Viceroy *, for the purpose
of repairing our water-casks, and landing the women to wash ; a dilapidated
monastery affording them and the marine guard a comfortable mansion.

* At 1l. a-day.

The

The entrance of the harbour of Rio
de Janeiro is narrow for about a quarter
of a mile ; it thence widens into a secure
basin, which at the town is five miles
in breadth, and extends inland beyond
the reach of the eye : several fruitful
islets are scattered on each side, which,
covered with loaded orange-trees, almost realize the fiction of the gardens
of the Hesperides.

The shores which surround the harbour are vastly mountainous, forming
abrupt and craggy precipices of the
most wild and extraordinary shapes.
Nature seems to have sported in the
formation of this her last work, and
to have combined all the fanciful forms,
which she scattered more sparingly over
the old continent. The entrance of the
7   har-

harbour is pointed out by a towering cliff, on the South side, rising perpendicularly from the sea ; while, at the head of the Port, the mountains rise into higher elevations, and present forms more strikingly singular ;

Rocks rich with gems, and mountains big with mines,
Whence many a bursting stream auriferous plays,

are here seen, now faintly peeping from behind the intervening clouds, and now presenting their dark blue summits above the flaky vapours that roll along their sides.

These mountains consist entirely of granite, forming an adamantine barrier to the waters of the ocean. They are clothed in every part where the least soil can remain, with trees and shrubs of various kinds ; and even to the naked rock,

rock, vegetables are seen to adhere, which appear to derive their nourishment from the moisture of the air alone. Here are many picturesque vallies, narrow, but winding along the base of the mountains, from the shores of the harbour to some distance inland. These glens are supereminently fruitful, from the combined causes of superior heat and moisture ; the first proceeding from the reflected heat of the sun, confined in a narrow space, and the latter produced by the condensation of the vapours, attracted by that heat, or driven by the winds against the mountains' sides. The numerous little coves at the entrance of these glens, are bordered with beaches of the finest sand, where fishermen have erected their dwellings, and which, viewing them from without,

have

have all the apparent neatness of our
best English villages; but too soon we
find, on entering them, that this is the
mere effect of white-wash, and that within, they are the habitations of sloth and
nastiness. The town of St. Sebastian
is built entirely of granite, which appears to be the only stone found here,
except a species of black and white
marble. From the Bay, the appearance of the town is not inelegant, but
the deception vanishes on a nearer approach. The streets, though straight
and regular, are narrow and dirty, the
projecting balconies sometimes nearly
meeting each other; the houses are
commonly two stories high, independent of the ground-floors, which are
occupied as shops or cellars; they are
dirty, hot, and inconvenient; the stair-

cases

cases are perpendicular, and without
any light; and in the arrangement of
the rooms, no regard is paid, either to
a free circulation of air, or to the
beauty of prospect. The furniture of
the houses, though costly, disgusts the
eye used to elegant plainness, by its
clumsiness and tawdry decorations;
while the spider weaves her web, and
pursues her sanguinary trade in uninter-
rupted security, upon the walls and ceil-
ing. In the houses of the rich, the
windows are glazed, which only serves
to increase the reflected power of the
sun, and render them intolerably hot;
but the generality of houses are furnished with shutters of close lattice-
work, behind which the women assemble in the evening; and while their
own persons are concealed, enjoy the
passing

passing breeze, which is not, however, always very aromatic. In the English Settlements within the tropics, art is exhausted to correct or mitigate the ardour of the climate, and to render a burning atmosphere, not only supportable, but pleasant to a northern constitution. In the Brasils the defects of climate are increased by the slothful and dirty customs of the inhabitants. The cause of this difference is to be ascribed to the climates of the mother-countries; the climate of Portugal approaching to that of Brasil, the Europeans who emigrate hither feel little inconvenience from the change; in our tropical Settlements, the climate of their old differing so much from that of their new residence, the emigrants leave no means unemployed to mitigate the fer-

vour

vour of the sun, whose ardent blaze is found to derange the nervous system, enervate the body, and render the mind a prey to listlessness and inanity.

There are eighteen parish-churches, four monasteries, and three convents in the town of St. Sebastian, besides several smaller religious buildings on the islands, and in the suburbs. Upon these edifices no expence is spared to attract the imagination of the weak and ignorant, by a profusion of gilding, and other tawdry decorations. The " Hopital de Mieseracordie" is also a religious institution, which receives patients of every denomination, and is principally supported by private benefactions. To these may be added a Penitentiary-House, where the incontinent fair are secluded

secluded from the world, to weep for,
and atone their faults in solitude and
silence; hither jealous husbands, or
cross parents, send their too amorous
wives and daughters, and doubtless,
often upon no better foundation, than
" trifles light as air." The admission
to the nunneries is expensive; and I
have heard a fond mother regret her
want of fortune, only because it prevented her dedicating some of her beloved daughters to God. The clergy
possess immense property, in land,
houses, and specie: when it was proposed to lay an impost of ten *per cent*
upon the income of the church, the Be-
nedictine monks offered to commute
their part of the tax, by paying 40,000
crowns annually. Their pious desire
for the conversion of heretics still glows

E   with

with all the ardour of bigotry, and the recantation of one protestant is considered of more value, than the conversion of 100 pagans; as in heaven there is more joy over one sinner that repenteth, than over ninety and nine just persons. An unfortunate foreigner of this persuasion, who by sickness, or other causes, is obliged to remain here after his ship sails, is continually plagued by the impertinent intrusion of a dozen of these pious fathers, who, if he can find no means of leaving the country, in general tire his patience out in a few months, and for quietness sake he consents to be saved according to their receipt *.

No

---

* In the library of the Autonian monks, we were shewn an English book, presented by Thomas Muir, with the following lines in a blank leaf:

Bib-

No foreigner is allowed to reside here, unless he subsists by some mechanical trade, or is in the service of the state; and if it appears that any idlers are inclined to remain in the colony by stealth, after sufficient warning and opportunities to get away, they are ar-

---

Bibliothecæ
Ordinis, Sancti Antonii Fratrum
Observantiæ suæ
THOMAS MUIR de Hunters-hill
Gente Scholus, Anima Orbis ferrarum Civis
Obtulit.

O Scholia ! ô longum felix, longumque superba
Ante alias patria, Heroum sanctissima tellus
Dives opum fecunda viris, lætissima campis
Ærumnus memorare tuas summamque malorum
    uberibus :
Quis queat, et dictis, nostra æquare dolores
Et turpes ignominias, et barbara jussa
Et nos patriæ fines, et dulcia linquimus arva,
Et cras ingens iterabimur æquor.
            Civitate Sancti Sebastiani 23 Julii 1794.

rested

rested and confined on Cobras Island, and either put on board their own country ships that may touch here, or sent to Lisbon as prisoners.

Besides the religious buildings, the other public edifices are the Viceroy's palace, which forms one side of a flagged square, fronting the landing-place: contiguous to this, and nearly adjoining each other, are the opera-house, the royal stables, the prison *, and the mint. The opera-house, which holds about six hundred persons, is open on Thursdays, Sundays, and most holidays: the pieces performed are, in-

---

In passing the prison, strangers are disgusted with the sight of half-starved and naked prisoners, with iron chains extending from their necks to the prison door, sufficiently long to admit their coming to the foot-path of the street, for the purpose of begging.

differently,

differently, tragedies, comedies, or operas, with interludes and after-pieces: the dialogue is in Portuguese, but the words and music of the songs are Italian. The house is wretchedly fitted up, the scenes miserably daubed, and where foliage is required, branches of *real* trees are introduced; so that while the artificial scenery wears the gay livery of summer, the natural sometimes presents the appearance of autumnal decay. The viceroy is expected by the populace, to shew himself at the theatre every night: on his entering the house, the audience rise, turn their faces towards his box, and again sit down. In private companies, no person sits while he stands, unless at his request; thus unsocial formality is the price that greatness every where pays for vulgar admiration.

E 3   The

The town is supplied with water from a hill by a lofty aqueduct, of two tier of brick arches, built in a light, and not inelegant style. The public garden, which contains between three and four acres of ground, is situated on the sea-side; the walks run in straight lines, and are shaded by mangoe trees, whose foliage is extremely luxuriant, and by its dark hue peculiarly calculated to refresh the eye, pained by the constant glare of the sun. At the extremity of the garden next the beach, is a flagged terrace, and a room hung with views of the country, and other curiosities; a fountain, which throws up a *jet d'eau*, waters the garden, and cools the air. In the winter, the garden is entirely deserted; the ladies then keep constantly in their houses, and the men, wanting that

that first inducement, the charms of female society, feel no inclination for a
barren promenade, but, following the
example of the fair sex, pass their time
in listless indolence, and, like the
swallow, remain in a state of torpidity
till the return of spring.

Those gradations of fortune, which
exist in, and indeed appear to be the
necessary consequences of a well-regu-
lated society, are not to be found in the
Brasils; the only distinction is the rich
and poor; the former are proud though
ignorant, and ostentatious though ava-
ricious; and the superabundance of all
the mere necessaries of life alone, prevents the latter from being indigent
beggars. Those who can acquire half

E 4   a do-

a dozen slaves, live in idleness upon the
wages of their labour, and stroll the
streets in all the solemnity of self-im-
portance. In their general expences, the
rich are penurious, and the marriage of
their children alone seems to thaw their
frozen generosity: on these occasions,
they run into the contrary extreme, and
ridiculous extravagance becomes the
order of the day. I have seen a bridal
chemise, the needle-work of which had
cost fifty pounds, and the rest of the
marriage paraphernalia was in the same
proportion of expence. Their entertain-
ments are profuse in proportion as they
are rare, but seldom possess any title
to elegance, and sometimes want even
common cleanliness to recommend them
to an English appetite *. The carriages

riages in use among the rich are cabrio-
lets, drawn by mules, and chairs cur-
tained round, in which they are carried
through the streets by Negro slaves;
the latter are also female conveyances.
Gaming, the peculiar vice of idleness, is
prevalent among the men. Pharaoh is

---

* In describing the manners of the Brasilians, it
will, I trust, be recollected, that I speak generally :
divested, as I hope I am, of national prejudice, I suppose the existence of an universal standard of social
manners, which, though very far from being arrived
at by any nation in the world, is more nearly approached by some than by others, and is perhaps
already reached by a few more happy individuals of
every nation. Among the Brasilians, though the general mass stand very low upon the fcale of refinement,
the proportion of these superior minds is, perhaps,
equal to what any other country can boast ; and I am
happy in bearing testimony, that at Rio de Janeiro,
refined hospitality, elegant taste, and politeness, devoid of formality, are the conspicuous characteristics
of several individuals.

their

their favourite game, and the fickle
Goddess is here pursued with as much
avidity as at Brooks's or Almack's; it is
but justice to the Brasilian ladies to
say, that they bear no part in this de-
structive vice, but whether from want
of inclination, or from restraint, I cannot take upon me to say.

The manners of the Brasilians are,
however, gradually converging towards
that liberal system, which appears to be
continually gaining ground throughout
the world, and which will probably be
one day universally established, in exact proportion to the peculiar physical
and moral attributes of man in the climate he inhabits. The usual dress of
both sexes is adopted from the French;
swords and cocked hats are entirely out
of

of fashion, and clokes are now only worn by the vulgar. The men who have had any intercourse with the English, adopt their customs, even to minuteness; hence, cropped heads, round hats, and half boots, have ceased to be considered a foreign costume. The women wear their waists very short, their bosoms much exposed, and their head-dresses and naked arms covered with a profusion of sparkling stones *, which are of little value here ; the ladies, however, as well as the men, seem to prefer attiring themselves *a la mode d'Angleterre*, when it is in their power. An English milliner who stopped here, on her way to India, performed greater metamorphoses on the external form of

* Topazes, aqua marinas, amethysts, and chriso-lites, &c.

some young ladies, than can be equalled
in the pages of Ovid *. The features
of the females can in no instance that
I saw, claim the title of beautiful, and
even very few deserve the epithet or
pretty: however, their black eyes,
large, full, and sparkling, give a degree
of brilliancy to their dark complexions,
and throw some expression into their
countenances; but it is too generally
the mere expression of animal vivacity,

---

* The amorous precepts of this author are well
followed by the Rio ladies;

> If *snowy-white* your neck; you still should wear
> That, and the shoulder of the left arm, bare;
> Such sights ne'er fail to fire my am'rous heart,
> And make me pant to kiss the naked part.
>
> ART OF LOVE, translated by Congreve.

But they should recollect, that this voluptuous author
addressed himself to Italian women, and that the
" Parian marble," to which their skins were com-
pared, is by no means applicable to Brasilian complexions.

untem-

untempered by the soft chastising
power of tender sensibility. Their eye-
brows are finely arched ; their eye-lashes
long and silken ; their hair is long, black,
and coarsely luxuriant ; and if we may
judge from the frequent application of the
fingers, is not always without inhabitants.
In their persons, they are unacquainted
with that delicate *properté*, from which
our countrywomen derive so large a
portion of their power over the other
sex, and for which they are conspicuous over all the nations of Europe. Among other habits of the
Brasilian ladies, which, separately considered, are perhaps trifling, but when
combined, form a powerful opposition
to the empire of female charms, is that
of continually spitting, without regard
either to manner, time, or place.

The

The young ladies who are educated
in the Convents, are permitted to con-
verse even with strangers at the gate,
and often shewed their partiality for
our countrymen, by the interchange
of pocket-handkerchiefs and other
trifles. There is something so interesting in the silvery tones of a secluded
damsel, when two rows of iron bars
intervene to prevent a near approach,
something so Pyramus and Thisbe*
like, that the heart of a true-born
Englishman cannot fail being cap-
tivated.

" 'Tis distance lends enchantment to
the view," and while he repeats the
swelling names of Magdelina, Antonia,

* Here Pyramus, there gentle Thisbe strove,
To catch each other's breath, the balmy breeze
of love.

OVID. MET.

or

or Seraphina, he deprecates the hell-invented barrier, that precludes him from imprinting the impassioned kiss on the hand of the sweetly pensive recluse. For the encouragement of my enamoured countrymen, who might otherwise give way to despondency, and pine in hopeless love, I cannot help informing them, that the iron bars of the convents are not quite so hard as adamant, nor the walls so high as to render an *escalade* impracticable; and that the watchful eye of the dragon, who guards the Hesperian fruit, has more than once been eluded by British ingenuity, or lulled to sleep by Brasilian gold.

The custom of dropping *bouquets* upon the heads of passengers, as signals

to

to assignation, is no longer to be found
at Rio, and as we have no reason to
doubt the veracity of the gentlemen *
who were thus favoured, we ought not
to pass over this alteration in the manners of the Brasilian women, without
endeavouring to account for it. Former travellers have always complained
of the difficulty they found in even
getting a transient view of women of
condition; this is, however, far from being the case at present: indeed, we generally found the manners of the ladies,
(particularly the unmarried ones) approaching nearer to the easy familiarity
of the English, than to the prudish reserve which is said to be the *exterior*
characteristic of Portuguese females.
As the manners of a people improve,

* See Capt. Cook's Voyage.

jealous

jealous restraints give way to delicate
attentions towards the females: men
begin to place confidence in women; and
the latter feeling their own importance,
soon acquire that proper pride which is
the great support of female virtue; and
enjoying the liberty of doing as they
choose, they think only of doing as they
ought. Thus secret assignations become
less necessary, as jealousy and scandal
cease to fetter the social intercourse of
the sexes; for experience proves the truth
of the remark, that virtue will ever be
displeasing, when she exhibits herself
only in the disguise of harshness, caprice, or some other repulsive quality.

In music and singing the Brasilians of
both sexes may be said to excel. These
are arts peculiarly congenial to luxurious

F   climates,

climates, for there the wants of man, being supplied by nature almost spontaneously, he has leisure to cultivate the soft impressions which the surrounding scenery creates, and by observing the harmonies of nature, he becomes a poet and musician. Dancing is a very favourite amusement, in which the ladies perform with extraordinary grace; besides national and English country dances, the native dance of the Indians is sometimes performed, the figures and motions of which are very little superior, in point of delicacy, to those of the Otaheitean timoradee.

The estimated proportion of the sexes at Rio is *eleven* women to *two* men; this may be attributed to physical as well as moral causes, for it is a demonstrable fact,

fact, that in warm climates more females
are born than males*; and secondly, the
females leading a life of seclusion and
temperance, and employed only in domestic offices, are entirely free from the
dangers, and but little subject to the
diseases which destroy the other sex.
While the men are occupied in the ha-
zardous pursuit of honour or of fortune
in distant countries, from whence they
are often doomed never to return, the
women are born and die without ever
quitting their paternal roof.

In the females of Brasil, as well as of
other countries in the torid zone, there

* Speculative writers have either doubted or denied
this assumption, but the observation of those who have
resided many years in Asia, fully authorize our stating
it as a " fact capable of demonstration."

is

is no resting time between the periods of
perfection and decline; like the delicate
fruits of the soil, the genial warmth of the
sun forces them to a premature ripeness,
and after a momentary bloom sinks them
towards decay: at fourteen they become
mothers, at sixteen the blossoms of their
beauty are full blown, and at twenty
they are withered like the faded rose in
autumn. Thus the lives of three of these
daughters of the sun are scarce equal to
that of one European ; among the former
the period of their bodily perfections far
precedes that of their mental ones, in
the latter they accompany each other
hand in hand. These principles, doubtless, influenced the wise law-givers of the
East in their permission of polygamy;
for, in the torrid zone, should a man be
circumscribed to one wife, he must pass
nearly

nearly two thirds of his days united to a disgusting mummy, useless to society, else the depravity of human nature, joined to the irritation of unsatisfied passions, would lead him to get rid of the incumberance by clandestine means. This confinement to a single wife, in the European settlements of Asia and America, is one of the principal causes of the unbounded licentiousness in the men, and the spirit of intrigue in the women. In the Brasils, the licentious intercourse of the sexes perhaps equals what we are told prevailed in the most degenerate period of Imperial Rome. The primary cause of this general corruption of manners, must be referred to climate, which acts forcibly in giving strength to the physical properties of love. In proportion as the passion for enjoyment is ex-

F 3   cited,

cited, the fear of losing the object which
confers it is increased, and hence proceeds the constitutional jealousy of men
in warm climates. In the Brasils, the
moment a girl is betrothed she becomes
subject to all the restraints imposed by
this rankling passion; and should the
absence of her intended husband be un-
avoidable, previous to the nuptial ceremony, he often causes her to be im-
mured within the walls of a convent till
his return. By such suspicions he too
often creates the evil he complains of,
and then punishes the crime he has pro-
voked; and while he thus becomes the ar-
biter of his own fate, he accuses Nature
of causing all his sufferings. Unmarried
females, being allowed much greater
liberties than wives, are by no means
anxious to be married, and consequently

1   neglect

neglect all those minute delicacies in their common intercourse with the other sex, which form the basis of mutual love, considered as a refined passion. But the climate operating upon the fair sex more forcibly in proportion to their superior delicacy of organization, enervates the system, and induces a kind of restless indolence, to which is attached a boundless desire for variety, when it can be procured without much exertion : hence, while the mind is lulled into inactivity, and the eye of prudence sleeps, the bosom is " tremblingly alive" to the soft sensations of love, and the bulwarks of female innocence lie exposed and defenceless to the attacks of the watchful seducer. The public opinion is not, however, so depraved as to *sanction* this laxity of morals, and hence pregnancy is

F 4   too

too often concealed by procuring abortion, which repeated, perhaps, several times, assists in bringing on a premature old age, and sinks the victim to the grave loaded with guilt and disease.

> Quod neque in Armeniis tigres secere latebris
> Perdere nec fœtus ausa Leæna suos.
> At teneræ faciunt, sed non impunè puellæ
> Sæpe, suos utero quæ necat, ipsa perit.
>
> OVID. AMOR. l. 2.

The punishment of adultery is transportation of both the offenders to different places on the coast of Africa; but the injured huſband may revenge himself by the instant death of both parties, if he finds them, " nudus cum nuda, solus cum sola."

The city of St. Sebastian, from being surrounded by hills, which prevent the free circulation of air, is more unhealthy than

than the other settlements on the coast,
and the dirty customs of the inhabitants
tend to increase the defects of situation.
The diseases most prevalent are fevers,
dysentery, and hydrocele. Fevers, if
not entirely generated, are undoubtedly
multiplied by the noxious effluvia arising from the unremoved filth in the
streets; for here the windows give a
nightly exit to all the vile accumulation
of the day *. Dysenteries may probably proceed from their method of living, or their common kinds of food, of
which fish, fruit, and sweetmeats, form
the principal articles. The chief animal

* For an exact description of St. Sebastian's in this
respect, we beg leave to refer our readers to Mrs.
Winifred Jenkins, and shall only remark, that who-
ever walks under the windows at ten o'clock at night,
will probably have occasion to cry, " Lord have mercy
upon me !"

food -

food of the lower-class is salted pork not
half cured, or jerked beef, both brought
from Rio Grande; and their beverage is
a deleterious and ardent spirit, which
from its cheapness comes within the
reach of their scanty finances. The
causes of the hydrocele, which often renders those afflicted with it the most piti-
able objects, may, perhaps, with equal
reason, be traced to themselves; for by
the continual use of tepid baths, they
increase the naturally great relaxation,
which pervades the system in a warm
climate. In our English settlements,
where cold bathing is daily practised,
such a disease is almost unknown *.
During the winter the thermometer seldom rises above 74°, and sometimes falls

* I know of but two other parts of the world where
this disease is greatly prevalent: at Cochin on the Coast
of Malabar, and in the island of Barbadoes.

to

to 65°. At this season heavy dews descend during the night, and the morn-
ings are enveloped in thick fogs, but
soon

> ———— The potent sun
> Melts into limpid air the high rais'd clouds,
> And morning fogs that hover'd round the hills,
> In party colour'd bands,

leaving the atmosphere pure and serene.
The land and sea breezes are tolerably
regular: the former commences towards
morning, and is commonly very light.
The sea breeze may be seen curling the
surface of the ocean at noon, but it
seldom reaches the town before two
o'clock: it is generally moderate, cool,
and refreshing.

The Creoles, at this season, seem to
feel all the effects of rigorous cold;
while

while we were melting in the lightest clothing, they muffled themselves up in their cloaks, and sat shivering, with their doors and windows closed. The rainy season commences in August; and for six weeks or two months, a continual torrent pours down, with a close and suffocating atmosphere. To the rains succeed the dry and parching months of November and December, when the Creoles are again re-animated; and awakened by the ardent blaze of the sun, from the lethargic torpidity of winter, renew their occupations or amusements.

CHAP.

CHAP. III.

Rio Janeiro.—Productions, Trade.—Slaves, Indians.—
Police and Courts of Juſtice.—State of Defence.—Po-
litical Situation.

THE chief vegetable productions of
the district of Rio de Janeiro are sugar,
coffee, cotton, cocoa, tobacco, and indigo;
of these, sugar is alone indigenous, and
was found growing wild by the first colonists. The tobacco raised in the Brasils is consumed there in segars and
snuff; and the cultivation of indigo has
been much neglected, since the East
Indian indigo has rivalled it in the European

ropean markets. The soil is every where
so rich, that it requires all the labour of
the farmer to check the too luxuriant
vegetation, and keep the ground free
from brush-wood and shrubs; a few
months' neglect covers the soil with a
tangled under-wood, bound together and
rendered impenetrable by creeping vines.
Twelve different kinds of oranges are
cultivated here, and all other tropical
fruits grow almost spontaneously; the
soil has also been found friendly to the
spices of the East, and pepper is already
cultivated with some success; in short,

Whatever blooms in torrid tracks appear,
Whose bright succession decks the varied year,
These here disporting own the kindred soil,
Nor ask luxuriance from the planter's toil.

The horses of Brasil are small, and incapable of much labour; in the interior
they

they run wild in vast droves, and are of so little value, that they are merely caught to perform a journey; and when tired, or the journey is over, are again turned loose. The mules, which graze in flocks about the town, are the chief beasts of burthen, and are particularly adapted to the precipices of the country. Oxen are brought from Rio Grande, where they are worth about eight shillings each, and where they are slaughtered merely for their hides and tallow; on their arrival at Rio Janeiro, though wretchedly impoverished by the journey, they are sold for fifty shillings to four pounds a-head. The farms are fenced by lime-bushes and orange-trees, intermixed with various flowering shrubs, equally beautiful and aromatic. At night, the trees appear illumi-

illuminated by myriads of fire-flies, which
play among the branches, for here

————On every hedge
The glow-worm lights his gem, and through the dark
A moving radiance twinkles.

The district of the mines commences
about sixty miles from Rio; their produce is conveyed thither on mules, es-
corted by detachments of cavalry, of
which there is a regiment stationed at
Minas, the Capital, which is said to be
large and populous; this province extends to the borders of the Spanish
settlements in Paraguay. The journey
to Matto Grosso, the farthest Portuguese station, is by Rio Grande, and is
said to take up six months in contending against the stream, but the return
is made in about three months; from
hence

hence comes the sarsaparilla and bal-
sam copaiba. The most minute precautions are taken to prevent the con-
cealment of diamonds, by persons of
every description coming from the
mines; they are not only stripped
naked, and minutely searched, but
even their horses and mules are *purged :*
this strict scrutiny sets ingenuity to
work to evade it, and the attempts are
often successful. A Friar coming from
the mines has been known to conceal
three superb diamonds, in the waxen
figure of the Virgin, which he carried
in his pocket; the superstition of his
examiners held the divine Image sacred, and kissing it with greater devo-
tion, than they would probably have
felt for the loveliest female of mere

G   flesh

flesh and blood, returned it to the holy
Father unexamined.

The King's tenth of the gold is taken
from the ore at the smelting-house,
where it is cast into ingots, which are
stamped, and then become a legal tender in payments ; if the owner wishes to
have it coined, it pays two and a half
per cent at the mint. The colonial gold
currency is in pieces of four millres,
or twenty-five shillings sterling; these
are greatly alloyed, to prevent their
exportation from the Colony. Most
of the gold sent to Portugal is
coined into half joes (2l.); and the exportation of uncoined gold is forbidden,
upon pain of transportation for life to
the coast of Guinea.

The

The Viceroy's salary is only about
2,600l. a-year, but, by perquisites, his
usual income amounts to between 15
and 20,000l. : these arise chiefly from
the sale of offices, which are all in-
vested in the Viceroy, and of which he
is said commonly to retain the third
part of the annual profits. His office
properly lasts only three years, but he
is generally continued until he has re-
alized a handsome fortune, for it is
usually the poor Grandees who are appointed to this lucrative government.
The present Viceroy is of the family of
Valencia, and related to the throne of
Portugal, by the house of Braganza;
he is a man of information, liberal and
polite in his manners, and apparently
attached to the English nation. The
vice-regal state is by no means equal to

G 2   that

that of our Indian Governor-General,
though their *supposed* incomes are nearly
the same.

That jealousy of foreigners which prevailed at Rio de Janeiro some years
ago, appears no longer to exist. We always found ourselves at perfect liberty
to make excursions as far as we chose,
either on foot, or on horseback, unat-
tended by any guard. This indulgence
however, appears to proceed from the
liberal sentiments of the Viceroy, and
was only extended to officers in the
King's service; and as the regulations
respecting foreigners are not abrogated,
they may be at any time put into execution with all their force. Upon the
eastern side of the harbour, we were
allowed to cut brooms, and wander
over

over the country in quest of game, without meeting the most distant interruption. Here, had any of *us** possessed botanical knowledge, or taste, we might have been abundantly gratified by the examination of plants, " beyond the power of Botanist to number up their tribes."

The improvement of the district of Rio de Janeiro, though it certainly does not equal what it might have been, if colonized by a nation of more persevering industry, may be looked on as rapid, under the torpidity of Portu guese indolence. Portugal has, however, possessed great advantages above all other nations of Europe, who have

* See Cook's Voyage.

colo-

colonized America, in having factories
on the opposite coast of Africa, whence
her colonists procure an easy, and continual supply of slaves. The mother-
country is so jealous of the rivalship of
the Colonies, that the introduction of
the most trifling manufactures is forbidden; the casting bells for the
churches, in particular, is laid under
severe penalties, lest the colonists
should one day learn, that bells and
cannon might be made from the same
materials.

None but professed merchants ever
think of turning their money to any account, by interest, &c.: many old misers
are known to have very large sums lying
dead in their coffers, which, for want of
banks, they keep in their own houses,
and

and live upon the wages of their slaves.
The trade of Rio de Janeiro, although
it has to contend with monopolies, pro-
hibitions, and a heavy duty of ten *per
cent*, but above all, with the unconquerable indolence of the Portuguese,
is by no means trifling, and is annually
increasing. It is confined entirely to
the mother-country, a direct trade with
foreigners, or by foreign ships, being
strictly prohibited. The fleets employed in the commerce of Brasil, are
confined to the ports of Lisbon and
Oporto, whence they sail and return
annually, in three fleets ; the great dis-
advantage of this method, however, begins to be seen by the merchants, and
single ships are at present allowed to
sail from Europe, without confinement
to any particular season. All foreign

vessels

vessels attempting to trade on the coast, are liable to confiscation; and a ship of the line, and two brigs of war are stationed at Rio, to support these commercial regulations.

The annual exports from the port of Rio Janeiro, are, from good authority, said to be as follows:

Exports.	Quantity.	Price at Rio.	Total value.
Sugar	13,000 chests of 15,00 cwt. each.	4d. per ℔.	£325,000
Rum [a]	5,000 leaguers of 150 galls. each.	15d. per gall.	46,875
Coffee [b]	800,000 lb. wt.	6d. per ℔.	40,000
Gold	400,000 half joes	2l. each	800,000
Silver [c]	70 0,000 Spanish dollars	5s. each	175,000
Raw Hides	3,000 tons		90,000
Rice	500 tons	25l. a ton	7,500
Cotton	800 tons	1s. per ℔.	89,600
Indigo	trifling, perhaps		10,000
Cochineal [e] Cocoa [f] Dye wood Drugs	variable, perhaps about		30,000
		Total value of Exports,	£1,613,975

[a] 200 leagues are sent to Angola for the purchase of slaves.

[b] In the year 1794, 40,000 lb. of coffee only was exported.

[c] This is sent to China and India. The Brasils have no silver mines, but procure it from the Spanish settlements in dollars: part is recoined into crown pieces for Colonial currency.

[d] Brought from Rio Grande.

[e] Procured from the Spanish settlements on the Rio Plata.

[f] Increasing.

About fifty ships, from three hundred to eight hundred tons each, sail annually from this port to Europe : these vessels

vessels are mostly built in the Brasils, the timber of which is said to equal the oak in durability. The imports are woollens, printed cottons, hard ware, cutlery, and wines, and, generally, all the articles necessary to the domestic economy of Europeans. The trade with Africa employs twenty-five ships, from one hundred and fifty to four hundred tons, who, in return for rum, gunpowder, arms, coarse cottons, and trinkets, import slaves, wax, and ivory, the latter of which, is re-exported to Europe. Corn and flour are brought from Rio Grande: one hundred and thirty vessels, from fifty to one hundred tons, are constantly employed in this trade, and in smuggling from the Spanish settlements; for the Spanish government at home, equally jealous with the Portuguese,

tuguese, strictly prohibits all foreign communication with its American colonies; hence arises (by the mutual connivance of the colonial governments) an extensive contraband trade, which, while it enriches individuals, diminishes the public revenue of both countries *.

Every article of merchandize, or consumption, whether the produce of the colony, or imported, pays to the crown a tenth part of its value, previous to its being exposed for sale. These duties

---

* The English East Indiamen and Whalers, who put into Rio Janeiro for refreshments, find a ready market for their private trade in piece-goods, hardware, hosiery, hats, porter, butter, and cheese. The Custom-house officers, and officers of the guard-boats, who constantly attend foreign merchant ships, conduct this trade with great ingenuity and address.

are

are generally farmed; and that on fish
alone produces 18,000 crowns annually.
The farmers of the revenue are autho-
rized to demand the assistance of the
military, if any resistance is made to its
collection. The whole amount of revenue raised in the district of Rio Janeiro,
is near four millions sterling.

The annual importation of negro
slaves, is said to amount to between
ten and twelve thousand; their value is
thus estimated: a full grown man 40*l*.,
a woman 32*l*., a boy 20*l*.; their value
is much increased, by their having had
the small-pox. The food of the slaves,
is Cassada bread, and Indian corn
roasted, and on the sea-coast some
fish. In the country, the owners are at
no expence for their diet: they allot
them

them a small piece of land, and a day in the week to cultivate it, and from it they are obliged to derive a subsistence for themselves and families. The plantation negroes are entirely naked; but in the towns, their owners have more regard to decency.

On the importation of a cargo of negroes, they are christened previous to their sale; for this purpose, they are marched to a church-yard, and separated into as many groups, as there are different names to be given : the priest standing in the middle of each group, flourishes a broom dipped in holy-water over their heads, until they are all well sprinkled, and, at the same time, bawls out to them, what their name is to be.

Most

Most of the imported negroes are sent
to the mines to replace those who have
fallen victims to their insalubrious atmosphere; many of them die shortly
after their arrival, from change of climate
and food, and a few from mental despondency, which is here degraded by
the name of sulkiness. Arguing from
the experience of two centuries, we shall
be almost induced to adopt the opinion
of Voltaire, that a physical cause can
alone produce so extraordinary an effect,
as an immense tribe kept in a state
of the most abject slavery by a handful
of foreigners, not amounting to the tenth
part of their own numbers. All the
false reasoning upon this subject may
be deduced from this fallacious maxim,
" that to judge correctly of the feelings
of others, we should suppose ourselves in
their

their situations;" but by placing ourselves thus, we do not judge of their feelings but of our own, and assume for granted what is contrary to nature, that man is every where the same. We do not consider that what to our constitutional energies and cultivated minds would appear the acmé of misery, may, to others of a different temperament, be a state of comparative enjoyment; for the perceptions of every individual being, create a standard of happiness in his own mind, and nature has given to no two the same capacity of enjoyment. If the negro inherited from nature the intellectual capacity of the European, why have we not seen him improve in the arts of civilization, by the force of natural ingenuity, or, at least, by the adoption of some of the knowledge of the latter. Here it

3 may

may be said, that his tyrannical masters deny him the means of acquiring that knowledge; but to answer this objection we need only enquire by what means many other people arose from barbarism, and we shall find ourselves obliged to trace back the road of improvement to original genius. The leaders of the negroes in St. Domingo may be adduced as instances of brilliant talents and unconquerable spirit in the sons of Africa; but rules are sometimes proved by their exceptions. A civil war, or a revolution in a state, opens an unbounded theatre for the exhibition of talents, and gives to native genius the power of distinguishing itself: we accordingly see it rising superior to all obstacles from want of education or political oppression. In the tumults of the

West

West Indies, a few leaders may be found,
who appear among their countrymen, a
kind of lusus naturæ, that more forcibly
point out their general degredation; in
fine, we may as well affirm, that education would give to the cart-horse the
spirit of a courser, or to the cur the
sagacity of the hound, as that it would
give to the negro the talents and abi-
lities of the European. But though
nature may deny to the sons of Africa
the *degree* of mental light which illuminates the western world, she has not totally forbidden them a participation in its
benign influence. Nature surely never
intended to create,

———Wretches born to work and weep
Explore the mine,

or, in short, to become the absolute property of other men; though she has not

H   raised

raised them to the standard of man in temperate climates, neither has she sunk them to the level of brutes; hence, although they are fitted to be more easily reduced to a state of subjection, they are not absolutely incapable of understanding the value of liberty, or ignorant of the means both of acquiring and preserving it. The negro is not always devoid of that courage and fortitude, that marks the superiority of his European tyrant: he suffers pain with the most stoical indifference, and often dares his master to punish him by inflicting tortures on himself. Many negroes retreat to the fastnesses in the mountains, where they form a body of implacable marauders, and warm with revenge, commit unceasing depredations upon the neighbouring farmers.

A short

A short time previous to our arrival,
an instance of heroism was exemplified in
a native negro, for which ancient Rome
would have erected him a statue next to
that of Virginius; and although my
pen is greatly incapable of doing justice
to the story, it would be still greater
injustice to suppress it.

The law obliges a master to give freedom to his slave, if the latter can procure the sum, at which he may be fairly
estimated; and this is almost the only
boon granted to this degraded race.

Senor D. was a wealthy planter in
the district of the mines, and among his
numerous slaves was one named Hanno,
who had been born on the estate, and
whose ingenuity had increased his value

H 2   much

much beyond that of his fellows. Scarce had Hanno arrived at that age when every zephyr seems the sigh of love, ere his fondest wishes centered on Zelida, a young female of his own age, and a slave to the same master; in her his partial eye perceived all that was beautiful in person, or amiable in mind; the passion was mutual, it had " grown with their growth, and strengthened with their strength ;" but Hanno, though a slave, possessed the feelings of a man, and his generous soul revolted at the idea of entailing that slavery upon his children, which was the only birth-right he inherited from his fathers. His mind was energetic, and his resolutions immutable: while he fulfilled his daily tafk, and was distinguished for his diligence and fidelity, he was enabled, by extra labour and the

utmost

utmost frugality, to lay by something,
without defrauding his master of his
time; and at the end of seven years, his
savings amounted to the estimated value
of a female slave. Time had not altered
his passion for Zelida, and they were
united by the simple and unartificial
bonds of mutual love. The absence of
Senor D. for two years prevented the
accomplishment of Hanno's first wishes,
the purchase of Zelida's freedom, and in
that time she had presented him with a
boy and a girl. Though slaves from
their birth, Hanno was not chagrined,
for he had now added to his hoard a
sufficient sum to purchase their liberty
likewise. On the return of Senor D.
Hanno anxiously demanded a compli-
ance with the law, but well aware of his
master's sordid avarice, cautiously af-

H 3   firmed,

firmed, that a kind friend was to advance him the money. Senor D. agreed to receive the price, and a day was fixed to execute the deeds before a magistrate. On that day Hanno fled upon the wings of hope to his master's house, while it may be supposed the most heartfelt joy animated his bosom, on the prospect of giving immediate liberty to those his soul doated on. He tendered the gold—it was seized as the stolen property of Senor D.; and Hanno being unable to bring forward the supposed lender, was condemned, and the cruelty of his master was exhausted in superintending his punishment. Still bleeding from the scourge, he returned to his hut, which, though the residence of slavery, had till now been cheered by the benign influence of love and hope. He found his

wife

wife suckling her infant daughter, while his son, yet unable to walk, was amusing her with his playful gambols upon the bare earth. Without answering Zelida's anxious enquiries, he thus addressed her: " To procure your liberty, more dear to me than my own, I have, since the moment of our acquaintance, deprived myself of every comfort my state of bondage allows; for that purpose, I have laboured during those permitted hours of relaxation, which my fellows have employed in amusements; I have curtailed my scanty meal of cassada, I have sold my morsel of tobacco*, and I have gone naked amidst the burning heats of summer, and the

---

* Tobacco is esteemed the greatest luxury next to rum by the negroes.

pinching

pinching colds of winter*. I had accomplished the object of all my cares,
and all my deprivations, and this morning I tendered to your owner the price
of your liberty, and that of your children; but when the deed was to be rati-
fied before the magistrate, he seized it
as his own, and accusing me of robbery,
inflicted the punishment of a crime my
soul detests. My efforts to procure your
liberty are abortive; the fruits of my
industry, like the labours of the silk-
worm, are gone to feed the luxury of
our tyrant; the blossoms of hope are
for ever blighted, and the wretched
Hanno's cup of misery is full. Yet, a

* The province of Brasil rises from the sea till it
reaches the summits of the Cordilleras, and the cold
necessarily increases in proportion to the ascent. The
district of the mines produces European fruits, and is
subject to frost.

way,

way, a sure, but dreadful way remains, to free you, my wife, from the scourge of tyranny, or the violation of lust, and to rescue you, my children, from the hands of an unfeeling monster, and from a life of unceasing wretchedness." Then seizing a knife, he plunged it into the bosom of his wife, and while reeking with her blood, buried it in the hearts of his children. When seized and interrogated, he answered with a manly tone of firmness, " I killed my wife and children to shorten a miserable existence in bondage, but I spared my own life to shew my brutal tyrant how easy it is to escape from his power, and how little the soul of a negro fears death or torment. I expect to suffer the utmost tortures that your cruelty can devise, but pain I despise thus, (staking his arm

on

on an iron spike, and tearing it through the flesh,) and death I desire, that I may rejoin my wife and children, who have, ere this, a habitation prepared for me in the land of our forefathers, where no cruel white man is permitted to enter." Even the proud apathy of the Portuguese was roused by this appeal to their feelings; the slave was pardoned and granted his freedom; Senor D. severely fined, and the unworthy magistrate, who seconded his villany, degraded from his office. I trust this digression will plead its own excuse, and shall conclude it with the hope, that the time is not far distant,

> Till the freed Indians, in their native groves,
> Reap their own fruits, and woo their sable loves.

The new negroes have an idea, that their priests can render them invulnerable

rable to the weapons of their enemies;
and hence arise the most bloody contests
between the different tribes, which the
severest punishments cannot suppress.
National hatred is one of the strongest
principles in the minds of the ignorant,
and a real John Bull as heartily despises
a Frenchman when fellow-prisoner as
when at liberty.

The native Indians in the district of
Rio Janeiro are few; the Portuguese
accuse them of aversion to any kind of
labour, and only employ them on the
water as boatmen. They are declared
by government entirely free, and their
conversion to Christianity is strictly ordered to be attempted by persuasion
alone. The missionaries are numerous,
and have so far succeeded in their spiritual

tual labours, that several towns of bap-
tised Indians are established in the district of the mines.

The harbour of Rio Janeiro is well
defended by forts and batteries on every
commanding position, which are garrisoned by about 4,000 regular troops,
who make a very respectable appearance, and seem to be extremely well
disciplined. The whites of every description, amounting to 10,000, are en-
rolled in a militia, and exercised once
a month. From this motley group, however, little service could be expected in
the hour of attack, and we might justly
exclaim,

'Twas not the spawn of such as these
That dar'd the elements on pathless seas,
And made proud Asian monarchs feel
How weak their gold was against Europe's steel;
But soldiers of another mould,
Rough, hardy, season'd, manly, bold.

With

Wite respect to the political relations
of the colony and the mother-country,
we may safely assert, that the bonds of
dependence have been drawn so tight
that they are almost ready to break.
The restraints on trade, the income-tax
of ten *per cent.* levied with the greatest
rigour, (a tax unknown in the English
colonies,) and the venality of those in
office, are glaring evils, which absolute
mental blindness could alone prevent
the Brasilians from seeing. The spirit
of discontent, which had been long
silently fermenting, openly shewed itself
a few mouths ago, upon an attempt to
introduce a stamp act into the colony :
this measure met with universal resistance from the colonists, who, to avoid
the penalties arising from non-compli-
ance, transacted all their money concerns

cerns *viva voce*, and upon honour*.
Should the irritated colonists be driven
to extremities, the mother-country will
probably find too late, that though a
disease at its commencement may be removed by gentle remedies, it will, by
neglect, soon grow too powerful for the
most desperate. The spirit of revolution
which, like the element of fire, seems to
pervade the habitable globe, at the present moment, is rapidly gaining strength
in these trans-atlantic regions. The
philosophy of Helvetius, Voltaire, Rous-
seau, and Volney, has here its admirers
and supporters, who only wait the favourable moment to kindle the latent
sparks into flame. These principles are
chiefly circulated and extended by a ma-
sonic society; which neither the despo-

* This act has since been carried into effect.

tic

tic power of the civil government, nor the denunciations of the church, have been able to suppress or control. In 1803, this society consisted only of twenty-five brethren ; in 1804, their numbers have increased to one hundred. Several officers of the inquisition have been sent from Portugal, to suppress it, but without effect; and the presence of these spiritual jackalls, creates but little uneasiness, as they possess no temporal authority, and can only send the culprits to Europe upon proof of their guilt. The French republic, which seems to neglect no means of revolutionizing every part of the globe, and to which force and intrigue are indifferent in this pursuit, have not forgotten the Brasils, where their emissaries are sufficiently active in the cause of anarchy

and

and confusion. The mother-country,
aware of the slippery tenure by which
the colony is held, with all the fears of
a weak despot, prohibits the erection of
a printing-press.

Should the Brasils revolt from their al-
legiance to the parent state, which in the
course of national events is by no means
improbable, and to which present ap-
pearances would authorize the fixing no
very distant period; the immense regions of Spanish America will doubtless
pursue the same steps. This region of
the globe appears, from its geographical
position, to be peculiarly adapted to the
growth of powerful states; while its natural divisions, and external aspect, are
eminently favourable to the preserva-
tion of liberty: for though, in its extent,

it

It occupies the whole of the torrid zone, from its great elevation it enjoys a more temperate climate than the southern provinces of Europe, and is consequently more congenial to freedom. Had South America been colonized by a northern people, who would have cherished the freedom they conveyed thither, it would at this day have presented a very different appearance.

CHAP. IV.

From Rio Janeiro to the Cape of Good Hope.—Islands of Tristan d'Acunha.—Cape Town.—Simmon's Town.— Dutch.—Departure from the Cape. — Island of St. Paul.—Arrival at Port Philip.

1803,
July. ON quitting the American coast under the tropic of Capricorn, the seaman takes leave of summer seas and gentle breezes for the rest of his voyage through the southern hemisphere; his care then consists in preparing his vessel to encounter the turbulent elements he is to meet with. But the storm which terrifies the landman into repentance, and vows of amendment, is welcomed by the experienced sailor, as expediting his passage; for he never considers how strong the wind is, while it continues

I 2   fair,

fair, and his bark is able to run before
it; or, if it is foul, he consoles himself
from day to day with the certainty, that
the longer it has continued so, the nearer
it is to a change. At this season the
prevailing winds, south of the parallel
of 36° S. are westerly, which often blow
with unabated violence for months together. The southern polar ices, which in
summer are often found floating in large
detached islands, as far as the latitude
of 37°, are in the winter bound together
or chained to the Antarctic rocks, and
thus they withstand the force of the
winds and currents; their neighbourhood is, however, evinced by the degree
of cold which gradually increases from
the tropic, till in the latitude of 40°,
where the thermometer falls to 50°, with
showers of sleet and hail.

Quitting

Quitting Rio Janeiro the 19th of July, with the wind at E. N. E. we shaped our course to the southward, in order to get into the region of westerly winds, which came on gradually till they fixed in strong N. W. gales. It was now found impossible to keep company with the Ocean, without running under bare poles, which strained the ship violently, and we therefore parted company near the Islands of Tristan d'Acunha; the largest of which we made on the 2d of August, The preceding evening it had blown a heavy gale, with a mountainous sea; but as we approached the island, the wind moderated to a fine breeze, the billows subsided, and the clouds clearing away, shewed the full-moon suspended in the clearest ether: by her friendly light, at about four o'clock we saw the

I 3   land,

land, at six leagues distance. As the dawn arose, the horizon becoming hazing, concealed it from our sight; but at sun-rise, the vapours again dispersing, left us a clear view of it till noon, when it was fourteen leagues distant.

The effect which the sight of the smallest spot of land, or even a bare uninhabited rock, has in breaking the tedious monotony of a long sea voyage, is easier felt than described. After passing a long succession of weary hours, with no other objects of contemplation than a world of waters, bounded only by the extent of vision, where it unites with the world of clouds, the sight of land acts like a talisman, and instantaneously transports us into the fairy regions of imagination. We compare the spot we

are

are viewing with one rendered inestima-
bly dear to us, by the remembrance of
its beloved objects, and the tender recol-
lection of past happiness. We pass over,
as points in time or space, the years or
seas that separate us; and by a cherished
delusion, find ourselves arrived at the
moment of re-union, cheered by the
embrace of friendship, or locked in the
arms of love and beauty.

The Island of Tristan d'Acunha, and
the circumstances attending our view of
it, brought forcibly to mind the beautiful apostrophé to Hope in Mr. Camp-
bel's poem.

> Angel of life, thy glitt'ring wings explore
> Earth's loneliest bounds, and ocean's wildest shore.
> Lo! to the wintry winds the pilot yields
> His bark careering o'er unfathom'd fields.
> Now on *Atlantic waves* he rides afar,
> Where Andes, giant of the western star,

I 4

With

With meteor standard to the winds unfurl'd,
Looks from his throne of clouds o'er half the world,
Now far he sweeps, where scarce a summer smiles
On Behrring's rocks, or Greenland's naked isles;
Cold on his midnight watch, the breezes blow
From wastes that slumber in eternal snow;
And waft across the waves' tumultuous roar,
The Wolf's long howl from Æonalaska's shore.

Poor child of danger, nursling of the storm,
Sad are the woes that wreck thy manly form;
Rocks, waves, and winds, the shatter'd bark delay,
Thy heart is sad, thy home is far away,

But hope can here her moon-light vigils keep,
And sing to charm the spirit of the deep;
Swift as yon streamer lights the stary pole,
Her visions warm the watchman's pensive soul.
His native hills, that rise in happier climes,
The grot that heard his song of other times,
His cottage home, his bark of slender sail,
His glassy lake, and broom-wood blossom'd vale,
Rush on his thought; he sweeps before the wind,
Treads the lov'd shore he sigh'd to leave behind,
Meets at each step a *friend's familiar face,*
And flies at last to Helen's long embrace,
Wipes from her cheek the rapture speaking tear,
And clasps with many a sigh his children dear!

While

While long neglected, but at length caress'd,
His faithful dog salutes the smiling guest,
Points to his master's eyes where'er they roam
His wistful face, and whines a welcome home.

These islands were discovered by the Portuguese, in their first voyages towards the Cape of Good Hope; they are three in number, the largest being that which we passed at the distance of two miles; it is almost bare of vegetation, but in one small spot on the north side, from whence a stream of water was observed precipitating itself into the sea: except in this place the north side of the island rises abruptly to a peak, the summit of which was at this time veiled by the clouds*. These islands abound in sea-

* When the wind is from the northward, the swell it must throw in on this side of the island, will hardly permit ships to anchor, or boats to land, without imminent danger. Its latitude we found to be 37° 9′ S., and longitude, by three chronometers, and a series of lunar observations (agreeing within ten miles), 11° 29′ 30″ E.

elephants,

elephants, whose oil is more valuable
than that of any other amphibious animal; and their tongues, when salted,
affords no despicable resource in a
scarcity of provisions *.

From Tristan d'Acunha a short run of
eleven days brought us off the Cape of
Good Hope, which we were in hopes of
passing with a continuance of our favourable wind; in this, however, we
were disappointed, as it suddenly veered
to the S. E. and obliged us to run to the

* This animal, to which sealers have given the name
of sea-elephant, appears to be the same as the sea-lion of
Anson, &c. The oil of the sea-elephant, by a simple
preparation, is found to answer the purpose of linseed oil
in painting. To *twenty* gallons of the oil, when boil-
ing, add " a quarter of a pound of white copperas,
two pounds of litharge or red lead, and half a pint of
spirit of turpentine;" after it has boiled half an hour
let it grow cold, pour the oil off from the sediment,
and it is fit for use.

north-

northward and make the land. Upon
mature deliberation it was thought better, under these circumstances, to run
into the Cape, than endanger the present high health of the ship's company
and convicts, by keeping the sea in this
stormy season; and we accordingly cast
anchor in Simmon's bay.

So much has already been written of
the Cape of Good Hope, by travellers
of every description, that little remains
to be gleaned by the most piercing observation. Different persons, however,
view the same objects in different points
of view, according to variety of disposi-
tion, or the temper of the moment; and
what may escape the general observer
in the wild field of nature, or be deemed
too trifling for the philosophic enquirer,

falls

falls to the lot of the humble gleaner﹔ and it is, indeed, by minute and familiar description alone, that we can point out to others the scenes that we ourselves have viewed.

Cape Town is one of the handsomest colonial towns in the world; the streets, which are wide and perfectly straight, are kept in the highest order, and planted with rows of oaks and firs. The houses are built in a stile of very superior elegance, and inside are in the cleanest and most regular order. They are not, however, sufficiently ventilated, to dissipate the stale fume of tobacco, which is peculiarly offensive to a stranger. The play-house is a neat building, erected by the English, where French and Dutch plays are acted alternately

ternately twice a week by private per-
formers.

The public garden, in which was
formerly a *mènagerie*, well stocked with
all the curious animals of Africa, was
entirely neglected by the English. Within the garden is the government-house,
a neat convenient building, without any
appearance of grandeur, and perfectly
consonant to the plain and frugal manners of the *old* Batavians. The torrents
which descend from the Table-hill in the
wet season often overflow the town; to
carry the waters off, canals are cut
through the principal streets, communicating with the ditch of the fort, and
thence with the sea.

Table and False Bay are separated by
an isthmus, which has evidently been

4   covered

covered by the sea at no very remote period, for it is a plain of fine sea-sand mixed
with shells, but little elevated above the
level of the sea. The S. E. wind, which
blows with great fury, forms this sand
into hills, which are in some places
bare, and in others bound by flowering
shrubs, and heaths of various kinds; the
distance between the two bays by land
is twenty-four miles. Quitting Simmon's
town, the road to Muisenbourg (a small
post about six miles from it) sometimes
runs along the beach which is flat, and
on which the sea flows with gentle un-
dulations; at others, it winds round the
feet of craggy hills, which are covered
with masses of stone suspended almost
in air, that seem nodding, and ready to
be displaced by the least impulse; even
the reverberation of sound, one would
think,

think, might dislodge them. The sides of these hills are covered with heath and shrubs, which throw out blossoms of every colour in the spring, and they abound in deer and other game. Regiments of baboons assemble on them, and, screened behind the impending rocks, roll down the loose masses on the passing traveller; wolves also descend from them in large troops, and " burning for blood; bony, and gaunt, and grim," seize as their prey the strayed oxen or wandering goats. A few scanty and turbid rills, apparently impregnated with iron, steal down the mountain's sides; but scarce a stream deserving the name of rivulet is to be found here. At Muisenbourg the road crosses a salt lake about half a mile wide, which is always fordable. From hence to within eight miles

of

of Cape Town, the road lies over a flat
heavy sand, where the path is distinguished only by the tracks of waggons; on either side the sand is covered
with an innumerable variety of flowering
heaths and shrubs, whose blossoms im-
pregnate the air, with the most balmy
odours. The remainder of the road to
Cape Town is formed of the iron-stone,
which abounds here, and is kept in excellent order. Neatly elegant country-
houses embellish it on each side, while
lofty oaks growing out of the fences,
and clumps of firs within them, in some
parts, give it the appearance of an English avenue. The entrance into the town
is over a down, rising on the left side
to the Table mountain, and on the right
descending to a fertile valley, with several neat farm-houses and wind-mills scattered

tered over it. The sides of the hills are variegated with patches of the silver-tree, contrasting their glossy leaves with the brown heath and barren rocks.

The sensations which possessed our minds on entering this beautiful town, fresh from sea, acquired the most vivid colours from contrast. The evening before we were confined to the narrow limits of a ship, surrounded and buffeted by the boisterous waves, and almost beaten down by the torrents of rain, mingled with the continual sprays of the sea; now the loud winds rending the sails, and whistling through the cordage, employed all our exertions to secure our vessel against its utmost fury; now incessant peals of thunder rattling above our heads, while after every vivid

K

flash

flash the eye felt a temporary suspension of sight, and the mind for a moment shuddered at the doubt of its total extinction, and recollected that a frail plank alone was the barrier between mortal existence and eternity. Now view the contrast in a few short hours; our vessel rides in safety where,

Smooth flow the waves, and zephyrs gently play,

while the danger and the fatigue past are drowned in oblivion; and now we tread the verdant turf, and breathe the balmy atmosphere of odoriferous flowers, while, as we approach the town, parties of equestrian ladies attract our eyes, attended by their beaux, whose happiness we might envy, did not the call of honour, and the voice of patriotism, render us *less* vulnerable to the charms

charms of beauty, or the blandishments
of love.

Simmon's Town is situated on a small
bay of that name, and contains about
one hundred and fifty well-built houses;
the inhabitants chiefly subsist by supplying ships with refreshments, during
the months they are unable to lay in
Table Bay. The English built a small
block-house, with a battery enbarbet, to
the eastward of the town; the post of
Muisenbourg has also a small battery,
and the beach, in places of easy access,
is guarded by a few guns. The road to
Muisenbourg has several difficult passes,
which might be defended against very
superior numbers. A detachment of
three hundred troops are stationed at Simmon's Town, who would, in the event of an

K 2   enemy's

enemy's landing, retreat to Cape Town, which is garrisoned by three thousand troops, chiefly Swiss, particularly the regiment of Waldeck, which having served under the English banner in the American war, remembers with partiality the food and pay of its old masters, both of which, in the Dutch service, are wretched enough.

The English, during the short period they were masters of the Cape, raised the price of every consumable commodity 200 *per cent.* but the Dutch government is again endeavouring to reduce things to their former level, and by the strictest economy to make the colony pay its expences. These measures are exceedingly unpopular, and have already caused upwards of one hundred

1   real

real or fictitious bankruptcies. Hence the partiality with which the English are viewed here. Their return is openly wished for, even by those who were formerly their greatest foes. In fact, the Dutch government at the Cape, as well as at home, is entirely under French influence ; and it is probable that in the boundless ambition of the Corsican usurper, he considers the Cape of Good Hope as one of the steps by which he intends to mount to Asiatic thrones.

The Dutch, as well as the English, who have any floating property in the colony, are anxious to remit it to England, and therefore bills bear a premium of from 30 to 35 *per cent.* for paper money, which is the only currency here, and which rises from 6d. to 100

rix-

rix-dollars *. A quantity of copper pennies were put into circulation by the English, but finding it difficult to adjust their intrinsic value to the currency of the colony, without confusion on the one hand, or loss to the importers on the other, it was determined to double their nominal value, by which government gained 60 *per cent.* at the same time their private importation was made penal.

In Simmon's bay the water is supplied to ships by cocks, at a wharf where boats may lay at most times. Firewood is the scarcest article here: this is owing to the parching S.E. winds preventing the growth of timber, except the silver-tree and pollard oak. The

* This was in August 1803.

car-

carriage between the two towns is by
waggons with fourteen or sixteen horses,
the hire of which is thirty-five rix-dollars
(6*l.* 2*s.*); the horses are small, but hardy,
and bear much fatigue. Oxen are also
used to draw the heavy waggons.

The women of the Cape, when *young*,
are often pretty, but whether from their
sendentary lives, or peculiar gross food,
in a few years they grow unwieldy, and
delicacy of shape is sunk beneath a load
of fat. Their dress is English, and in
this respect the severe sentence of Ovid
on the fair sex in general, is peculiarly
applicable to the Cape ladies;

Pars minima est, ipsa puella sui.

The contrast between a gay, attentive, and well-dressed English officer,

K 4   and

and a grumbling, coarse, and phlegma-
tic Dutchman, was too obvious not to
strike the Batavian fair ones, and their
partiality was so openly expressed, that
our countrymen could not well avoid
taking advantage of it, and in pure
compassion, preventing them from
" wasting their sweetness on the desert
air." But, in this respect, public opinion seems to be at present the only
criterion of right and wrong, and as that
opinion is entirely governed by the conduct of the majority, such venial tres-
passes are considered with mutual cha-
rity, and the damsel who takes an annual trip to the country for the benefit
of *mountain* air, returns in about *two*
months, and receives the congratulations
of her friends upon the restored bloom
of her complexion, with the modest
air

air of a vestal " as chaste as unsunned snow."

In contemplating the manners and opinions of different nations, we are often apt to attribute to the caprice of the human mind, effects which proceed from natural causes alone, over which man can scarcely be allowed to possess any influence. The cleanliness and industry of the Dutch form a striking contrast with the dirt and indolence of the Portuguese, but are not more opposite than the climates of Holland and Portugal. The religious sentiments of these two nations are not less different than their external manners, and may, perhaps, be ultimately deduced from the same cause. At Rio Janeiro, the lofty spires of innumerable churches arise in every

every point of view; the streets are
crowded with priests of every denomination and habit; the air continually re-
verberates the solemn sounds of the
cloyster bell, while the harmonious notes
of the vesperal hymn, chaunted in slow
cadence, breaks the silence of the evening, and forces reverence from the bosom
of levity itself.   At the Cape of Good
Hope, two churches and two clergymen
are enough for the inhabitants, and at
Simmon's Town there is no trace of the
peculiar appropriation of the sabbath to
religious duties ; all here are employed
in making money.   Money is the su-
preme divinity of a Dutchman, for which
he would renounce his religion, sell his
wife, or betray his friend.

The slaves at the Cape are either Mo-
sambique negroes or Malays from the
eastern

eastern Archipelago, and we must do their masters the justice to say, that they are more humane in their treatment of them than any other European nation. When in fear of punishment, the slaves often retire to the Table mountain, and give much trouble to the police.

Having secured the continuance of our people's health, by the daily supply of fresh beef and bread, and having received on board five cows, one bull, and twelve sheep for the new Settlement, we put to sea on the 25th, with a fine breeze from the N. W. to the expected continuance of which we trusted for an expeditious passage to the coast of New Holland, and accordingly steered to the southward, to get into the supposed range of its greatest strength. In these south-

southern seas, we were continually surrounded by whales, and were even sometimes obliged to alter our course to avoid
striking on them. They often visit the
bays about the Cape, and while they
sport on the surface, the winds and
waves carry them so near the beach, that
all their exertions are insufficient to ex-
tricate themselves, and they perish on
the shore. Their blubber is removed
and converted into oil by persons who
farm this prerogative from government.
Flocks of albatrosses, and various kinds
of peterals, follow the whales, and feed
on the oily substances which they exude.

On quitting the Cape, it was natural
for the reflecting mind to recur back to
the history of the first adventurous navigators who passed this formidable barrier

rier to ancient navigation. Comparing our own situation and views with those of De Gama and his followers, we are led to appreciate, as it deserves, their persevering boldness, while our admiration is excited by the progress of human invention and improvement, so peculiarly exemplified in the art of navigation.

The stormy seas which wash the southern promontory of Africa, (to which was then given the appropriate name of " Cap de las Tormentos,") are despised by the British seamen, whose vessel flies in security before the tempest, and while she " rides on the billows and defies the storm," he carelessly sings as if unconscious of the warring elements around him. In the revolution of all sublunary affairs,

affairs, when the past and the present
arc alike sunk in the oblivious abyss of
time, when De Gama is no more heard
of, and a faint tradition alone records
the doubtful power and opulence of
the British isles, then shall some other
transcendent genius arise, who, braving
this foaming ocean with equal difficulty
and equal glory, shall claim the honour
of a first discoverer.

———Venient annis
Secula seris; quibus oceanus
Vincula rerum laxet, et ingens
Pateat tellus, Typhisque novos
Deteget orbes; nec sit terris
Ultima Thule.　　　　SENECA MEDEA.

Scarce had we cleared the land, ere
the favourable wind left us, and veering
to the eastward, continued to blow from
that quarter for eleven days; but by the
assistance

assitance of strong easterly currents*, we were enabled to preserve our distance from the land. The constant wet and cold weather which now prevailed, required every care and attention to obviate its evil effects upon the convicts, many of whom, through mere carelessness when in fine weather, were now literally naked; the taylors were, therefore, employed in making up jackets and trowsers, from the materials sent on board for the purpose, which were distributed to those most in want. Slight dysenteries were for some time prevalent, but by the unremitting care of the surgeon, and the most minute attention to keeping the prisons well aired and dry, as well as to the personal cleanliness of the convicts, one man only

* Vide Addenda I.

fell

fell a victim to this disease. The incle-
ment weather had a more fatal effect
on the colonial cattle, three of the heifers
dying shortly after we left the Cape.

It was our intention to make the
island of St. Paul's, in order to verify
our chronometers*, which were at this
period

---

* The chronometers on board were constructed by
Mr. Mudge, N° 8, and N° 12. The rate given in
England continued without variation to Tristan d'A-
cunha, but in the run from thence to the Cape we
found an error of half a degree of longitude, that is,
a *loss* of two minutes of time. On the 29th of August,
N° 8 stopped without any apparent cause, and the next
day resumed its going; this prevented any dependence
being placed on it for the rest of the passage. At Port
Philip and Port Jackson, the rates were again ascertained
by daily observations, and they continued to agree, until
a few days after leaving Port Jackson, when N° 8
again stopped. N° 12 agreed perfectly with the land-
fall of Cape Horn, but on our arrival at Rio Janeiro we
found

period no less than six degrees a-head of the reckoning, but night having overtaken us, and the wind blowing fresh and fair, we ran past them in the dark; our vicinity was, however, evinced in the morning, by large patches of rock-weed, the leaves of which were very broad, and resembled in shape those of the sycamore *

From

---

found an error of 75 miles of longitude to the westward, being a loss of five minutes of time from Port Jackson to Rio, for the given longitude of Cape Horn could not be depended on.

* The confounding the names of the islands of St Paul and Amsterdam, which has been the case since Capt. Cook's voyage, as well as the uncertainty of their relative situations, must cause some uneasiness to the navigator in passing them of a bad night. A Dutch Captain at the Cape asserted, that they were only twelve miles distant north and south of each other (but I presume he must have meant Dutch miles, equal to English leagues).

L   Malham's

From the island of St. Paul to the Coast of New Holland, the winds were commonly between the N. W. and S. W. and our track was confined to the pa-

---

Malham's Naval Gazette of 1801 places St. Paul's in latitude 37° 56′, longitude 77° 22′, and makes Amsterdam in 36° 40′; 75° 15′. To make this agree with the other calculations, there must be an error of the press of two degrees in the latter latitude, which would then be 38° 40′; that is, 44′ difference.

Mr. Bowdich, who is in general the most correct in the latitudes and longitudes of places, takes the mean of Capt. Bligh's and Sir Geo. Staunton's observations, and makes the islands in the same longitude, viz. 77° 11′, and St. Paul's in latitude 37° 52′, and Amsterdam in 38° 42′, 50′ difference.

Mr. Maſkelyne, in his requisite tables, says, St. Paul's (meaning, I suppose, the Amsterdam of the others,) is in latitude 38° 44′, longitude 77° 18′.

Hamilton Moor makes St. Paul's in latitude 37° 31′, and longitude 77° 56′, and Amsterdam in 38° 15′, and 78° 00′. Upon the whole it appears, that the northernmost island is about the latitude of 37° 55′, and the southernmost 38° 40′.

rallels

rallels of 38° and 39°; with the wind
from the northward, we always found
the sea remarkably smooth, but when
the southerly wind prevailed, the heavy
swell, even in light breezes, evinced the
long fetch of the waters, and demon-
strated the general tempestuous weather in the high southern latitudes.
These circumstances alone would be
almost sufficient to refute the opinion
of a southern continent, did not the
voyages of Capt. Cook put it beyond
a doubt.

From the longitude of 125° E. the
oceanic birds, which before flitted over
the waves in vast numbers, began to decrease, and in 137° scarce one was seen.
This being the spring of the southern
hemisphere, they, doubtless, now retire

L 2   to

to the rocks, to deposit their eggs and raise their young.

On Saturday, October 10th, we at last made King Island *, in the entrance of Bass's Straits, which we had anxiously looked out for the two preceding days; the wind being from the N. E. obliged us to stand within three miles of the island, which through the haze we observed to be moderately high and level, with three sandy hills nearly in the centre. The increasing breeze and lowering sky, which portended a coming gale, prevented our examining the island more minutely. Fortunately we stood off in time to gain a sufficient offing before the gale com-

* Named after P. G. King, Esq. the present Governor of New South Wales.

menced,

menced, which during the night blew a
perfect hurricane between the N. W.
and S. W. This night of danger and
anxiety, was succeeded by a morning
beautifully serene, which shewed us the
southern coast of New South Wales.
From the total want of information respecting the appearance of the land on
this coast, we were doubtful as to our
situation, and approached the shore with
cautious diffidence; at length the break
in the land, which forms the entrance of
Port Philip, was observed, but a surf,
apparently breaking across it *, created,
at first, some mistrust of its identity,
until the man at the mast-head observing

---

* This we afterwards found was occasioned by the
rapidity of the ebb-tide, counteracted by the wind,
which created a breaking sea, that must destroy the
best constructed open boat.

a ship

a ship at anchor within, which was soon
recognized for the Ocean, removed all
doubt, and without farther hesitation we
pushed in for the entrance. A fair wind
and tide soon carried us through; and in
a few minutes we were presented with a
picture highly contrasted with the scene
we had lately contemplated: an ex-
panse of water bounded in many places
only by the horizon, and unruffled as
the bosom of unpolluted innocence,
presented itself to the charmed eye,
which roamed over it in silent admiration. The nearer shores, along which
the ship glided at the distance of a
mile, afforded the most exquisite scenery,
and recalled the idea of " Nature in
the world's first spring." In short,
every circumstance combined to im-
press our minds with the highest satis-
faction

faction for our safe arrival, and in creating those emotions which diffused themselves in thanksgiving to that Almighty Guide, who conducted us through the pathless ocean, to the spot of our destination.

CHAP. V.

Transactions at Port Philip from the Arrival to the Sailing of the Calcutta.—Survey of the Port.—Natives.— Communication with Port Jackson.—Determination to remove the Colony.—Examination of Western Port.

THE week following our arrival at Port Philip was occupied in searching for an eligible place to fix the settlement. As it was of the first consequence that this should be of easy access to shipping, the shores near the mouth of the port were first examined. Here, to our great mortification, we observed a total want of fresh water, and found the soil so extremely light and sandy as to deny all hopes of successful cultivation. As it was, however, determined

to

to land the people, a small bay, eight miles from the harbour's mouth, was pitched upon for that purpose, where, by sinking casks, water of a tolerable quality was procured, and here the camp was pitched; and on the 16th of October, the marines and convicts were landed, while the ships immediately began to discharge their cargoes.

On the first days of our landing, previous to the general debarkation, Capt. Woodriff, Colonel Collins, and the First Lieutenant of the Calcutta had some interviews with the natives, who came to the boats entirely unarmed, and without the smallest symptom of apprehension; presents of blankets, biscuit, &c. were given to them, with which, except in one instance, they departed satisfied and inoffensive.

The

The wash streak of the boat striking one of their fancies, he seized it and threw it behind the bushes; to shew him the impropriety of this, the blankets which had before been given them were taken away, and they were made to understand, that they would not be restored until the board was brought back by him who conveyed it away: this, after some delay and much reluctance, was at last done.

Though the vicinity of the harbour's mouth afforded no situation calculated for the establishment of the colony, it was naturally expected from the extent of the port, (its extremes being sunk in the horizon,) that convenient spots might be found; and the First Lieutenant of the Calcutta, with two boats, was directed

directed to ascertain this material point, by as careful a survey of the port as time would permit. From the reports of this survey, made to Capt. Woodriff, the following descriptive particulars are extracted.

Port Philip lies in the bottom of a deep bight between Cape Albany Otway and Point Schank. Coming from the westward, the Port may be known by a single bluff head-land without trees, rising from low land, thickly wooded, about four leagues to the westward of the entrance, to which we gave the name of Whale-head, from its resemblance to that fish. The prevalence of southerly winds renders Port Philip easily accessible, but in the same proportion the egress is difficult, for Point

Schank

Schank bearing S. E. and Cape Otway
S. W. it is obvious that with the wind
at south a ship would not clear either,
and the heavy swell that constantly
tumbles on the coast between Port
Philip and Western Port, will often
render it impossible (particularly in light
winds) to keep off the shore, which here
presents a continued barrier of rock,
that denies the smallest hopes of escape
to those dashed upon it.

The face of the country bordering on
the port is beautifully picturesque, swelling into gentle elevations of the brighest
verdure, and dotted with trees; as if
planted by the hand of taste; while the
ground is covered with a profusion of
flowers of every colour; in short, the
external appearance of the country flat-
tered

tered us into the most delusive dreams of fruitfulness and plenty.

The soil (except in a few places where marle is found mixed with vegetable mould,) is invariably sandy, and its blackness proceeds from the ashes of the burnt grass, which has every where been set fire to by the natives. The proportion of sand varies, and in some spots the soil may be sufficiently strong to produce vegetables, and, perhaps, Indian corn; but it may safely be asserted, that (excepting a few acres at the head of the port) no spot within five miles of the water will produce wheat or any other grain that requires either much moisture or good soil. On some of the highest elevations an arid sea-sand is found, giving nourishment to no other vegetable

vegetable than heath and fern. The
bases of the hills consist of very coarse
granite, which is here found in every
stage of formation, from grains scarcely
adhering, and crumbling into sand between the fingers, to the perfect stone
which almost defies the chissel.

The great scarcity of water is one of
the greatest disadvantages the port labours under. In the narrow glens between the hills, the marks of water-
courses are visible, but at this time
(October) they are mostly dried up;
pools of fresh water are found scattered
about the port, but they are merely
drains from swamps, and from their
stagnation are strongly impregnated with
decayed vegetable substances.

On the eastern side of the port, twenty-eight miles from the entrance, a stream of fresh water empties itself into the port. This stream runs through an extensive swamp, and appears to be a branch from a large river, at the northern extremity of the port, which the shortness of time and badness of the weather prevented our examining. The bed of this stream is covered with foliaceous mica, which our people at first conceived to be gold dust, and thence expected they had discovered an Elsatedorado.

On the west side of the port is an extensive lagoon, the water of which is too shoal to admit even small boats but at full tides; and in several places salt lagoons are found, generally closed by

2   the

the beach, where ducks, teal, and swans
are found in abundance.

The timber, within five miles of the
beach, is chiefly the she-oak, which is
only fit for cabinet work; the trees are
open, and the country is entirely free
from under-wood, except in the swamps,
which are always covered with an impenetrable brush. The other kinds of
timber trees are very thinly scattered
within the above limits; they are the
blue-gum, stringy-bark, honeysuckle,
box, and a kind of pine; of these the
three first grow to a large size, and when
sound, would probably be useful in ship-
building. From the lightness of the soil,
as well as its want of depth, the trees
shoot their roots horizontally, and having no hold of the ground, are blown

M   down

down in great numbers by every strong wind.

Of potable vegetables, wild celery, wild parsnip, scurvy-grass, and samphire, were found in great abundance, and several other kinds were eaten by our people *. The only fruits we found were the cone of the she-oak, which, when green, has a pleasantly acid taste, and a small berry, called by the colonists the Port Jackson cherry.

The kangaroo is the largest animal yet discovered in New Holland; it inhabits the neighbourhood of Port Philip in considerable numbers, weighing from 50 to 150 lb.; the native dog, the opossum, flying squirrel, and field-rat make

* Vide Addenda II.

up

up the catalogue of animals we observed.

Aquatic birds are found in abundance
on the lagoons, and are black swans,
ducks, teal, black and pied shags, peli-
cans, gulls, red-bills (a beach bird), he-
rons, curlews, and sand larks; the land
birds are eagles, crows, ravens, quail,
bronze-winged pigeons, and many beautiful varieties of the parrot tribe, particularly the large black cockatoo; the emue
is also a native of this part of the country,
its eggs having been found here. Three
varieties of snakes were observed, all of
which appeared to be venomous. The
species of insects are almost innumerable: among them are upwards of one
hundred and fifty different kinds of
beautiful moths; several kinds of beetles,

the

the animated straw, &c. The swamps
are inhabited by myriads of musquitoes
of an extraordinary size; but the common fly, which swarms almost beyond
belief, possesses all the offensive powers
of the musquitoe, its sting creating an
equal degree of pain and inflammation.
Wasps are also common, but no bees
were seen.

Fish, it may safely be asserted, is so
scarce that it could never be depended
on as a source of effectual relief in the
event of scarcity. Several varieties
of the ray were almost the only ones
caught, with sometimes a few mullet,
and other small fish; in general, a day's
work with the seine produced scarcely a
good dish of fish. The number of sharks
which infest the harbour may occasion
this

this scarcity of small fish. The rocks outside the harbour's mouth are frequented by seals and sea-elephants. The shell-fish are oysters, limpits, mussels, escalops, cockles, sea-ears; and very large cray-fish are found among the rocks.

Deeming minerals, as well as limestone, coal, and clays, of the greatest consequence to the colony, particular attention was paid to searching for them; the only appearance of minerals was in large masses of iron-stone, in some specimens of which, the shape, colour, and weight seemed to authorise the conclusion of its richness*. Lime-stone was

* From this stone, when pulverized, the natives, I suppose, procure the red earth with which they paint their faces.

M 3

found in many places, but the search for
coal was fruitless. Several kinds of clay
fit for pottery, bricks, &c. were found in
abundance, but always, more or less,
mixed with sand; indeed, after displacing
a thin covering of sand and ashes, the
bottom, in most places, was found to be
a soft friable sand-stone of a yellowish
colour.

With respect to climate, we had not
sufficient time to judge of its effects on
the human constitution; the vicissitudes
of heat and cold are very great, the thermometer varying from 50° to 96°, between sun-rise and noon of the same day;
and on the 19th and 21st of October it
froze pretty smartly at the head of the
port. The N. W. winds, which come on
in violent squalls, have all the disagreeable effects of the sirocco of the Levant,
but

but seldom last more than an hour, when the wind returns to the S. W. with thunder, lightning, and rain*.

The N. W. side of the port, where a level plain extends to the northward as far as the horizon, appears to be by far the most populous; at this place, upwards of two hundred natives assembled round the surveying boats, and their obviously hostile intentions made the application of fire-arms absolutely necessary to repel them, by which one native was killed, and two or three wounded. Previous to this time, several interviews had been held with separate parties, at different places, during which the most friendly intercourse was maintained, and endeavoured to be strength-

* Vide Addenda III.

M 4   ened

ened on our part, by presents of blankets, beads, &c. At these interviews they appeared to have a perfect knowledge of the use of fire-arms; and as they seemed terrified even at the sight of them, they were kept entirely out of view. The last interview which terminated so unexpectedly hostile, had at its commencement the same friendly appearance. Three natives, unarmed, came to the boats, and received fish, bread, and blankets. Feeling no apprehension from three naked and unarmed savages, the First Lieutenant proceeded with one boat to continue the survey, while the other boat's crew remained on shore to dress dinner and procure water. The moment the first boat disappeared the three natives took leave, and in less than an hour returned with forty more, head-

ed

ed by a chief who seemed to possess much authority. This party immediately divided, some taking off the attention of the people who had charge of the tent, (in which was Mr. Harris the surveyor of the colony,) while the rest surrounded the boats, the oars, masts, and sails of which were used in erecting the tent. Their intention to plunder was immediately visible, and all the exertions of the boat's crew were insufficient to prevent their possessing themselves of a tomahawk, an ax, and a saw. In this situation, as it was impossible to get the boat away, every thing belonging to her being on shore, it was thought advisable to temporise, and wait the return of the other boat, without having recourse to fire-arms, if it could possibly be avoided ; and for this

purpose,

purpose, bread, meat, and blankets were given them. These condescensions, however, seemed only to increase their boldness, and their numbers having been augmented by the junction of two other parties, amounted to more than two hundred. At this critical time the other boat came in sight, and observing the crowd and tumult at the tent, pushed towards them with all possible dispatch. Upon approaching the shore, the unusual warlike appearance of the natives was immediately observed, and as they seemed to have entire possession of the tent, serious apprehensions were entertained for Mr. Harris and two of the boat's crew, who it was noticed were not at the boat. At the moment that the grapnel was hove out of the Lieutenant's boat, to prevent her taking the ground, one

of

of the natives seized the master's mate,
who had charge of the other boat, and
held him fast in his arms, a general cry
of " Fire, Sir; for God's sake, fire!" was
now addressed from those on shore to
the First Lieutenant. Hoping the report only would sufficiently intimidate
them, two muskets were fired over
their heads; for a moment they seemed
to pause, and a few retreated behind
the trees, but immediately returned,
clapping their hands, and shouting ve-
hemently. Four musquets with buck
shot, and the fowling-pieces of the gentlemen with small shot, were now fired
among them, and from a general howl,
very different from their former shouts,
many were supposed to be struck. This
discharge created a general panic, and
leaving their cloaks behind, they ran in
every

every direction among the trees. It was hoped the business would have terminated here, and orders were, therefore, given to strike the tent, and prepare to quit the territory of such disagreeable neighbours. While thus employed, a large party were seen again assembling behind a hill, at the foot of which was our tent: they advanced in a compact body to the brow of the hill, every individual armed with a spear, and some, who appeared to be attendants of others, carrying bundles of them; when within an hundred yards of us they halted, and the chief, with one attendant, came down to the tent, and spoke with great vehemence, holding a very large war spear in a position for throwing. The First Lieutenant, wishing to restore peace if possible, laid down his gun, and ad-

vancing

vancing to the chief, presented him with
several cloaks, necklaces, and spears,
which had been left behind on their
retreat; the chief took his own cloak
and necklace, and gave the others to his
attendant. His countenance and ges-
tures all this time betrayed more of
anger than fear, and his spear appeared
every moment upon the point of quitting
his hand. When the cloaks were all
given up, the body on the hill began to
descend, shouting and flourishing their
spears. Our people were immediately
drawn up, and ordered to present their
musquets loaded with ball, while a last
attempt was made to convince the chief,
that if his people continued to approach
they would be immediately fired upon.
These threats were either not properly
understood, or were despised, and it was

4 deemed

deemed absolutely necessary for our own safety, to prove the power of our fire-arms, before they came near enough to injure us with their spears; selecting one of the foremost, who appeared to be most violent, as a proper example, three musquets were fired at him at fifty yards distance, two of which took effect, and he fell dead on the spot, the chief turning round at the report saw him fall, and immediately fled among the trees, a general dispersion succeeded, and the dead body was left behind.

Among these savages, gradations of rank could be distinctly traced, founded most probably upon personal qualities and external appearance. In these respects the chief far excelled the rest; his figure was masculine and well-propor-tioned,

tioned, and his.air bold and commanding.
When first he was seen approaching the
boat, he was raised upon the shoulders
of two men, and surrounded by the
whole party, shouting and clapping their
hands. Besides his cloak, which was
only distinguished by its superior size,
he wore a necklace of reeds, and several
strings of human hair over his breast.
His head was adorned with a coronet of
the wing-feathers of the swan, very neatly
aranged, and which had a pleasing effect.
The faces of several were painted with
red, white, and yellow clays *, and others
had

* In viewing the manners of man in his most savage
state, in which a cultivated mind sees only disgusting
images of wretchedness, we yet cannot fail to notice that
universal principle, which seems to act with equal force
upon the refined courtier of Europe and the wandering
savage of the desert. The Parisian beau cannot take
greater pains in adjusting his hair, or perfuming himself

had a reed or bone ran through the sep-
tum of the nose, perhaps increasing in
length according to rank, for the chief's
was by far the longest, and must have
measured at least two feet. Ornamental
scars on the shoulders were general, and the
face of one was deeply pitted as if from
the small-pox, though that disease is not

---

self with the odours of the East, than the savage does
in bedaubing his face with clays, or anointing his skin
with the blubber of the whale. To carry the proof yet
farther, we find that savages who are unacquainted
with the adventitious ornaments of dress, have recourse
to various methods of altering the natural forms of the
limbs or features, or to marking the body with scars,
punctures, &c. which they deem highly ornamental.
Among some tribes the head is flattened, among others
it is rendered more convex, but the nose and ears are
the chief objects of their personal vanity, and among all
the savage tribes I have seen, they undergo some kind
of distortion. As these operations are performed in
infancy, when the parts are flexible, and capable of
taking any form, we are often led to conclude, that to
be the natural configuration, which is only the effect of
artificial distortion.

known

known to exist in New Holland *. A
very great difference was observed in
the comparative cleanliness of these
savages; some of them were so abo-
minably beastly, that it required the
strongest stomach to look on them without nausea, while others were sufficiently

* Two attempts have been made to convey the vac-
cine matter to New South Wales, one by the Glatton,
and the other by the Calcutta, but both failed of success. Are we certain that any advantage would have
accrued from the introduction of such a disorder into
the colony? Hear what a celebrated writer says on
this subject : " Distempers, local in their origin, become more formidable when transplanted, than in their
native soil; the small-pox, so little feared in Europe,
almost depopulated America, and the plague is much
more inveterate when it invades Europe, than in its
native East. This is easily accounted for; the human
frame is prepared by custom and by climate for the
admission of the native disease, which is not the case
where it is transported." What opinion would we
form of an attempt to introduce a new disease into
England, merely to prevent the evils attending the
possible introduction of the plague!

N   cleanly

cleanly to be viewed without disgust.
The beards, which are remarkably bushy,
in the former were allowed to grow,
while in the latter they were cut close,
apparently by a sharp instrument, probably a shell.

The only covering they make use of,
to preserve their persons from the winter's cold, is a square cloak of opossum
skins, neatly sewed together, and thrown
loosely over their shoulders; the fleshy
side, which is worn inwards, is marked
with parallel lines, forming squares, lo-
zenges, &c. and sometimes with un-
couth human figures in the attitudes of
dancing.

Their arms are spears, used with a
throwing stick, like those of Port Jackson;

son; their shields are made of a hard wood and neatly carved; their war-spears are barbed with pieces of white spar, or shark's teeth, fastened on with red gum, and within a certain distance must be very dangerous offensive weapons. Their fish-gigs are pointed with the bone of the kangaroo, and with them they strike the rays which lay in shoal water. We saw no fish-hooks, nor other implements for fishing in deep water, nor any appearance of canoe, or other water conveyance *. Their food consists chiefly of shell-fish, and their ingenuity in procuring more substantial aliment, seems confined to the construction of a rude trap, upon the projecting points of the harbour, where the water-fowl lighting

* I have since been informed, that canoes were found on the river at the head of the port.

at

at night are entangled and caught-
The scarcity of food must at times reduce them to great extremities. If they
ever quit the vicinity of the water, their
sole subsistence must be on lizards,
grubs, and the few opossums they may
be able to kill; for the kangaroo, both
by its activity and wariness, I should
suppose to be out of the reach of their
weapons, or their ingenuity. The skins
of these animals having never been seen
with the natives corroborates this opinion, and it is probable, that the bones
with which their fish-gigs are pointed,
are those of animals which have died a
natural death. That they scruple not to
eat lizards and grubs, as well as a very
large worm found in the gum-trees, we
had ocular demonstration; indeed the
latter they seem to consider a very great

3   deli-

delicacy. Bread, beef, and fish, which they received from us, they devoured with great eagerness, swallowing large pieces without chewing, as if afraid of its being taken from them, but in no instance could we get them to drink. Spirits they appeared to dislike from the smell alone, and sweet punch they would taste and spit out again with disapprobation. They chew the green leaves of various plants, several of which had a slight astringent taste, and an aromatic smell.

Their huts merely serve the purpose of temporary shelter from the weather. They are constructed of branches of trees placed slanting and open on one side, which is always to leeward; if a fallen tree is near, it usually serves to support the hut, and sometimes when coarse

N 3   grass

grass is convenient, it is interwoven with the branches. Their fires are made at the very entrance of the huts, and if the wind shifts must be immediately re-moved. We had no opportunity of ob-serving their method of first kindling a fire, as the parties we saw had always a fire-brand with them, by which, and a little dry grass, they soon made a " roar-ing blaze."

The only traces of society we could observe, was in a cluster of five huts, near which a well of brackish water was probably the only inducement to so close a neighbourhood. How they supply themselves with water in ge-neral we were at a loss to guess, for, upon the closest examination, none was found within several miles of the
place

place where they had constructed their huts.

We had a sufficient proof of their burying their dead, by finding a human skeleton three feet under ground, while digging for water; its decayed state evinced its having been in the ground long before the arrival of any European at this port.

The only domestic utensil observed among them was a straw basket, made with tolerable neatness. Their cookery is confined to broiling, in which they are not very delicate; for the fish they sometimes received from us were put on the fire, and devoured without the useless preparation of gutting, cleaning, &c. Blankets they received with much satis-

N 4   faction;

faction; but though several to whom they were given paid us visits afterwards, their blankets were always left behind, and they presented themselves shivering with cold. This manœuvre might probably have been intended to induce a repetition of the gift, unless we suppose them to have been given to their women, which would argue a degree of civilization, from which they are immeasurably removed. Though in our first interviews they seemed to be stupidly devoid of curiosity, and viewed our persons and boats with the most perfect indifference, yet their latter conduct shews, that many of our conveniences appeared valuable, and fear was at last found much more powerful in deterring them from appropriating those things to themselves, than any idea of right or wrong.

The

The natives of this part of New South
Wales appear to differ very little from
those in the vicinity of Po t Jackson;
the same cast of features bespeaks the
same origin; their arms, their ornaments, and their dances, are much alike,
and they seem to differ only in language,
and in the ceremony of knocking out
a front tooth of every male, those of
Port Philip having their jaws perfect.
One woman only was seen, who retired
by desire of the men on our approach,
and one boy paid us a visit, from whose
conduct we could not infer the existence
of a great degree of subordination,
founded on difference of age; this
youngster was more loquacious and
troublesome than the men.

Nothing could offer a more perfect
picture of reposing solitude, than the
wilds

wilds of Port Philip on our first arrival.
Here Contemplation, with her musing
sister Melancholy, might find an undisturbed retreat. Often at the calm hour
of evening I have wandered through the
woods,

> Where the rude ax with heaved stroke
> Was never heard the nymphs to daunt,
> Or fright them from their hallow'd haunts.

The last hymn of the feathered choir-
isters to the setting sun, and the soft
murmurs of the breeze, faintly broke the
death-like silence that reigned around;
while the lightly trodden path of the soli-
tary savage, or the dead ashes of his fire,
alone pointed out the existence of human
beings. In the course of a very few
weeks the scene was greatly altered;
lanes were cut in the woods for the passage of the timber carriages; the huts

of

of the woodmen were erected beneath
the sheltering branches of the lofty trees;
the " busy hum" of their voices, and
the sound of their axes, reverberating
through the woods, denoted the exertions of social industry, and the labours
of civilization. At other times, sitting
on the carriage of a gun, in front of the
camp, I have contemplated with succeeding emotions of pity, laughter, and
astonishment, the scene before me.
When I viewed so many of my fellow-
men, sunk, some of them from a rank
in life, equal or superior to my own,
and by their crimes degraded to a level
with the basest of mankind; when I saw
them *naked*, wading to their shoulders
in water to unlade the boats, while a
burning sun struck its meridian rays
upon their uncovered heads, or yoked to
and

and sweating under a timber carriage, the wheels of which were sunk up to the axle in sand, I only considered their hapless lot, and the remembrance of of their vices was for a moment absorbed in the greatness of their punishment; I exclaimed with enthusiasm,

> 'Tis liberty alone that gives the flower
> Of fleeting life its lustre and perfume,
> And we are weeds without it.

When, on the other hand, I viewed the lively appearance of the camp, the employments of the women, and the ridiculous dilemmas into which they were every moment thrown by the novelty of their situations, I smiled, and inwardly admiring the pliability of mind, which enables us to accommodate ourselves to the vicissitudes of fortune, confessed that the pride of independence, and the

keen

keen sensibility of prosperity, like marks
imprinted on the sand, are soon effaced
by the current of adverse circumstances.
What once seemed more valuable than
life itself, even female virtue, grows
weaker by degrees, and at last falls a
sacrifice to present convenience; so true
is the poet's exclamation, that " want will
perjure the ne'er-touch'd vestal."

And now again, when I considered the
motives; when I contrasted the powers,
the ingenuity, and the resources of ci-
vilized man, with the weakness, the ignorance, and the wants of the savage he
came to dispossess, I acknowledged the
immensity of human intelligence, and
felt thankful for the small portion dis-
pensed to myself. These thoughts naturally led to the contemplation of future

ture possibilities. I beheld a second Rome, rising from a coalition of banditti. I beheld it giving laws to the world, and superlative in arms and in arts, looking down with proud superiority upon the barbarous nations of the northern hemisphere; thus running over the airy visions of empire, wealth, and glory, I wandered amidst the delusions of imagination.

The unfavourable account given of Port Philip, by the First Lieutenant of the Calcutta, immediately presented the necessity of removing the colony to a more eligible situation, but from a total want of knowledge respecting any recent discoveries, which might have been made on the neighbouring coasts, it was deemed necessary to receive instructions

on

on this head from the Governor in Chief at Port Jackson. The Ocean transport, being now discharged, was to proceed on her voyage to China, and could not, therefore, be detained without a heavy expence to government. Thus the only means left of communicating with Port Jackson was by an open boat; a six oared cutter was accordingly fitted for the purpose, in which Mr. Collins (who came out on a sealing speculation) undertook to convey the Lieutenant Governor's dispatches. After being nine days at sea, and encountering much bad weather, he was picked up by the Ocean (who sailed six days after him), within sixty miles of Port Jackson, and by her conveyed thither. Governor King, from a correct survey of Port Philip, made by Mr. Grimes, the Surveyor-General of
the

the Colony, was already convinced of its
ineligibility for a settlement, and immediately chartered the Ocean to remove
the establishment, either to Port Dalrymple, on the north side of Van Diemen's land, or to the river Derwent, on
the south coast of the same island,
where a small party from Port Jackson
was already established.

As the farther detention of the Calcutta, after the removal was finally con-
cluded on, would greatly retard the
principal object of her voyage, the con-
veying a cargo of ship timber to England, without any adequate advantage
to the Colony, she quitted Port Philip
on the 18th of December, leaving the
Colonists preparing to re-embark on
board the Ocean.

While

While the Calcutta remained at Port Philip, besides the necessary duties of the ship, the crew were actively employed in collecting such specimens of ship-timber as the place afforded; and about one hundred and fifty pieces of compass-timber, chiefly honeysuckle, were procured *.

During the period of uncertainty, between the sailing of the boat, and the return of advices from Port Jackson, the First Lieutenant of the Calcutta, with several other officers, and a party of convicts to carry provisons, proceeded by land to examine Western Port †, and ascertain the correctness of the description given of it

* Vide Addenda, Nº IV.

† Western Port was discovered by Lieutenant Flinders, in 1799.

O   by

by the first discoverers, particularly with respect to coal, in which it was said to abound. From the camp we proceeded across the peninsula to where the ridge of Arthur's Seat descends to the sea. This peninsula is formed entirely of sand, thrown up into round hillocks, and covered with coarse grass in tufts; the only trees here are the she-oak, which are small and open. After passing the ridge of Arthur's Seat we proceeded in a direction due east, nearly parallel to the sea-shore, of which we sometimes came in sight, until we reached a point projecting into the sea, which we supposed to be Cape or Point Schank; in this space the land continues to rise, and forms in larger and steeper hills, separated by narrow glens, but the soil is still very sandy, and no

water

water is to be found, even by digging in the hollows several feet deep. After passing: Cape Schank, the country immediately assumes a quite different appearance; the soil changes to a stiff clay; the she-oak gives place to the blue gum, and two strong runs of water fall into the sea immediately under the Cape. Here we halted for the night, and, following the example of the natives, erected a hut, and made a fire within a few feet of its entrance. This point we supposed to be twenty-five miles distant from the camp. At day-light we again commenced our march, guided by a pocket-compass; and keeping at the distance of between three and five miles from the sea at noon reached Western Port, about two miles from its entrance. From Cape Schank the coun-

try

try is varied by hills and vallies, the soil of the former being a stiff clay, with very lofty gum-trees ; and of the latter, a rich black mould several feet deep, except in a few spots where a black peaty earth was found. The grass in these vallies is extremely luxuriant; some of them are over-grown with under-wood, while others possess scarce a single shrub. In this track are several small runs of water, emptying themselves into the sea by deep ravines.

Our examination of Western Port was unavoidably confined to the space of a few miles on the western shore; this was principally owing to the man who carried the whole of our bread, having absconded soon after quitting the camp, and to our being deceived in the

the extent of the Port, as well as the distance to it; which we found much greater than we had any idea of.

We were provisioned only for four days, at short allowance; for trusting to our guns for an addition to our fare, we employed most of the party to carry water, being ignorant whether any was to be found in our route.

From the entrance of the Port for about twelve miles along the western shore, there is but one place of commodious landing for boats; the beach being either a black plate rock, or a flat sand running out a quarter of a mile; upon which a long and dangerous surf continually breaks. There are three good runs of water in this space, which

O 3   falling

falling from the hills, form pools at their base, and are absorbed by the soft sand of the beach. We found these pools covered with teal of a beautiful plumage, and, what was to us of much more importance, of a delicious flavour.

As our track to Western Port had never diverged more than five miles from the sea, it was determined, on returning, to endeavour to penetrate through the country in a N. W. direction, which we supposed would bring us to Port Philip at about twenty miles distance from the camp. We accordingly set off at daylight of the third day, from our night's station, which was about five miles from the entrance of Western Port, and had scarce walked a quarter of a mile when we came to an immense forest of lofty gum-

gum-trees. The country here becomes
very mountainous: in the vallies or rather chasms between the mountains,
small runs of water trickle through an
almost impenetrable jungle of prickly
shrubs, bound together by creeping
plants. After passing eight of these
deep chasms in six miles, which was
accomplished with infinite difficulty
in four hours, we found the country
grow still more impenetrable, vast fields
of shrub as prickly as furze arresting our
progress every moment. Several of our
people who carried the water, being unable to bear the fatigue any longer, we
were obliged to give up our intention;
and after a short rest, we shaped our
course to the S. W. in order to approach
the sea, where the country becomes
open and less hilly. In this direction

O 4   we

we found the country well-watered, the
soil very rich, and in many places mea-
dows of from fifty to an hundred acres,
covered with grass five feet high, and
unincumbered with a single tree. At
sun-set we reached the sea at Cape
Schank, and, halting for the night, arrived at the camp in the afternoon of the
next day.

Our search for coal, which we were
given to understand abounded at Western Port, was fruitless ; but our examination was too circumscribed and super-
ficial to authorize any positive assertion
respecting it.

The coast between the ridge of Arthur's Seat and Western Port is bound
by rocks of black stone, which was
found

found to burn to a strong lime. The projecting points of land are high, bluff, and perpendicular, presenting a barrier to the sea which breaks against them, even in the finest weather, with violence, denying shelter by anchorage, or safety by running on shore for the smallest boat.

Besides herds of kangaroos, four large wolves were seen at Western Port. Very beautiful bronze-winged pigeons with black and white cockatoos, and innumerable parrots, inhabit the woods.

Though this excursion added but little to the knowledge of the country, it is hoped it will not be entirely devoid of utility. In those spots which appeared best adapted to the purpose, seeds from
Rio

Rio Janeiro and the Cape were sown, viz. oranges, limes, melons, pumpkins, Indian corn, and several kinds of garden seeds.

But two huts were found in our track, and not a native was seen ; indeed the kangaroo seéms to reign undisturbed lord of the soil, a dominion which, by the evacuation of Port Philip, he is likely to retain for ages.

Several convicts absconded from the camp soon after their landing, led away by the most delusive ideas of reaching Port Jackson, or getting on board some whaler, which they ignorantly believed occasionally touched on this coast ; some of them were brought back by parties sent after them, and others returned voluntarily,

luntarily, when nearly famished with hunger. Two only of these unfortunate beings were never heard of after leaving the camp, one of these was George Lee, a character well known to several persons of respectability in England.

After the Calcutta quitted Port Philip, a vessel was sent to examine Port Dalrymple; the accounts brought back not being so favourable as was hoped for, it was finally determined to remove the Colony to the river Darwent, which was partly accomplished before the Calcutta sailed from Port Jackson. The name of Hobart was given to the Settlement, and the most flattering accounts were received from the Lieutenant Governor, of the situation, soil, and climate. Speaking of the climate, he says, that it may

be

be considered the Montpelier of New South Wales.

The remainder of the Calcutta's voyage was almost totally barren of incident, either to amuse or instruct. She sailed from Port Philip the 18th of December, and passing through Bass's Straits, without experiencing any difficulties, arrived at Port Jackson the 26th. Here she took in a cargo of ship-timber (about six hundred logs) and sailed again on the 17th March 1804; passed to the southward of New Zealand, which was seen on the 29th; doubled Cape Horn on the 27th April, and arrived at Rio de Janeiro the 22d May; thus accomplishing a voyage round the world, discharging and receiving a cargo, in eleven months.

In

In the long navigation between New Zealand and Cape Horn, scarce a single incident occurred either to interest the seaman, or the naturalist. Throughout this navigation, the wind seldom deviated to the northward of N. W. or to the southward of S. W. with strong gales, which enabled us to make an average of one hundred and eighty miles a-day for twenty-nine days.

The variety and numbers of austral oceanic birds, which followed our track, was very great; and it was remarked, that they were seen in greatest numbers during stormy weather. It is probable that the winds at those times disturbing the waters to their utmost depths, may bring blubbers and other substances, up-on which these birds feed, to the sur-face

face in greater quantities. In fine weather they probably retire to the rocks*,
where such food may then be most plen-
tiful.

Among these birds we chiefly noticed
the albatross, black shear-water, sooty
petrell,. pintado birds, Port Egmont

* The existence of many undiscovered islands, rocks,
and shoals in the southern ocean, may be inferred from
several circumstances. The patches of sea-weed met
with many hundred leagues from any known land is
one of them, and the frequent temporary smoothness
of the sea without any apparent cause is another. The
Bounty Islands, in the latitude of 47° 32′ S. and longitude 179° 10′ E. were accidentally discovered by
Captain Bligh, and an island was found in latitude
49° 19′ S. and longitude 179° 20′ E. by Captain Water-
house, to which he gave the name of Pen-antipode.
Neither of these islands were examined. Would it
not be an object worthy of the attention of the British
government, to employ a vessel in traversing these seas
during the summer months, in order to acquire a greater
certainty on this head?

6   hens,

hens, small grey gulls, and mother
Cary's chicken.

On the 3d April, in latitude 48½° S.
and longitude 186½° E. at 9 P. M. a
bright orange glow was observed in the
heavens to the southward; it rose from
the horizon to the altitude of thirty degrees, having the appearance of the.
western sky, when the sun in summer
illuminates it after setting. This appearance lasted about an hour, anc
gradually sunk into the surrounding ob-
scurity.

The Calcutta passed between the
islands of Diego Ramirez and the Her-
mits, and at about six miles distance
from the former. The strength of the
wind prevented our sounding here, but
from

from the muddiness of the water we judged it could not be above thirty fathoms deep : here we found a very strong current setting to the S. E. Diego Ramirez, which is laid down in several charts as one island, on the contrary consists of two detached groups of rocky islets, bearing N. by W. and S. by E. from each other. The passage between the groups is about three miles wide, and (as I was informed by the master of a whaler) is clear of danger. Scarce any vegetation is found on them, the naked rock being every where visible. Cape Horn we passed at the distance of four leagues, and observed several patches of snow on its sides; the wind was at west, and the thermometer as high as forty-eight, with very pleasant clear weather. From the appearance of the Hermit's islands

we

we conjectured that they must afford
many good harbours. The day after
rounding Cape Horn, we passed Staten
Land, of which we had a complete view
from end to end, than which nothing could
appear more desolate and unfriendly.

Off the coast of Patagonia three land-
birds lighted on board, and were caught;
the body resembled that of the crow, its
length eighteen inches, the bill one
inch and a half, the feathers of the
head forming a bunch over the fore-
head, the plumage a beautiful snowy
white, the legs and claws black. When
caught, they almost immediately became domesticated, and fed on meat.
They lived about six weeks, and appeared to be killed by the excessive
heat of the weather *.

* These appear to be the birds described by Captain
Cook.

P   After

After passing Cape Horn, the sea was at times covered with luminous blubbers about nine inches long, which emitted a light equal to that of a wax candle; it was observed, that the appearance of these blubbers always foretold the approach of stormy weather.

At Rio de Janeiro we recruited our water, and sailed again on the 1st of June.

We now once more turned our thoughts towards the shores, which custom and reason bid us hail as the happiest of our globe. Blest isle! where liberty is the birth-right of man; where the laws are the protectors, not the oppressors, of freedom; where beauty is crowned by modesty, and love is refined

by

by delicacy! And shall that freedom bow to the yoke of Gallic slavery? Shall those laws be changed for the arbitrary dictates of Gallic despotism? Shall that beauty be polluted by the unhallowed touch of ferocious invaders? and that love be degraded into the sensual appetite of brutes? No! the arms of Britons will be nerved with tenfold strength, for the protection of such inestimable blessings, and the insatiate foe will at last be convinced that

Britons never will be slaves.

P 2

ADDENDA.

N° I.

(Page 143.)

THOUGH the currents of the ocean have long occupied the attention of scientific men, no general theory has yet been found to answer under all circumstances. It may, I think, be assumed that oceanic currents depend upon principles as fixed as those to which we refer the currents of air; and also, that heat and cold operate in like manner upon both ; to these causes may be added the influence of the heavenly bodies, and it is therefore to be regretted, that navigators have never thought of comparing with accuracy the changes and courses of currents with the revolutions of the sun and planets. Colonel Capper observes, that " the currents in the northern Indian ocean, the gulf of Sind, and the bay of Bengal, almost invariably take the same course

as

as the wind. The cause of this connection between the wind and water seems almost to speak
for itself; from the vernal to the autumnal
equinox, that is, during the S. W. monsoon,
the lower current of air, and also the waters of
the southern hemisphere are put in motion, to fill
up a vacuity, caused by the rarefaction of the
atmosphere, and the evaporation of the waters of
the northern atmosphere, both of which are increased near the land. And on the contrary,
from the autumnal to the vernal equinox, when
the sun is on his return to the tropic of Capricorn,
the atmosphere being rarified over every part of
the southern hemisphere, the wind and water
operated on by the same causes, will move in a
contrary direction from the N. E. to the S. W.
As a confirmation of this hypothesis, currents
are always found in proportion to the strength of
wind, and both the winds and currents grow
weaker towards each equinox." The currents
running to the northward in the Indian ocean,
between the vernal and autumnal equinoxes, may

also

also be strengthened by the fusion of the southern polar ices, during the southern summer solstice; and this will operate, though in a diminishing ratio, until the sun reaches the equator on his return to the southern hemisphere. See St. Pierre's Theory of Currents in " Les Etudes de la Nature."

N° II.

(Page 162.)

List of Plants found at Port Philip, October, November, and December, 1803.

BROOKLIME.
Lesser Celandine.
Everlasting, several varieties of.
Indigo. Indigo fera ulatissima. Lin.
Flax.
Thistles, several species of.
Dandelion.
Devil's bit Scabious.
Plantain Rebwort.
Trefoil, several species of.
Catmint.
Veronica Spike, a variety of, bearing white
  flowers.
Geranium, several species of.
Heaths, several beautiful species and varieties.

Convol-

Convolvulus.

Wild Parsley.

Vetchling, several species of.

Samphire, several species of.

Hottentot Fig.

Kangaroo Grass.

Quake Grass, and several species found in England.

Oxye Daisy.

Black Knapweed.

Yarrow.

Nettle.

Wild Parsnip.

—— Celery.

—— Raspberry.

Chrysanthum.

Fern, several varieties of.

No III.
(Page 167.)

Meteorological Journal for the Months of October, November, and December, at Port Philip.

Days.	Thermometer.		Winds.	Weather.			Remarks.
	Sun rise.	Noon.		Morning.	Noon.	Night.	
Oct. 11	68	70	S. S. E.	clear pl.	str. br.	calm	
12	74	76	S. W.	fair	str. br. clo.	rain	
13	59	65	S. W.	clo. rain	str. br. clo.	str. br.	
14	59	59	S. W. W.	str. br. clo.	li. br. rain	fair	
15	64	64	W. N.	fair	fair	fair	
16	66	66	E. S. E. S. E.	fair	str. br. clo.	fair	
17	72	76	S. E.	fair	fair	fair	
18	58	64	S. E. S.	fair	fair	fair	
19	74	80	E. S. W.	fair	cloudy	fair	
20	68	70	variable, calm	fair	fair	fair	
21	66	66	variable, calm	fair	fair	fair	
22	74	74	E. S. S. W.	fair	fair	fair	

23	76	76	S. S. W.	fair	str. br. clo.	fair	Severe thunder and lightning, and heavy rain at 8 P.M.
24	76	76	S. S. W. W.	fair	fair	fair	
25	60	64	calms	fair	fair	fair	
26	59	60	calm	fair	fair	fair	
27	71	71	W. W. by S.	fair	cloudy	fair	
28	67	67	S. W. S.	fair	fair	fair	
29	69	69	S.	squally	fair	fair	
30	73	74	N.	rain	cloudy	cloudy	
31	—	—	S. W.	dark gl.	cloudy	squally	
Nov. 1	70	76	W. S. W.	str. br. rain	rain	rain	
2	72	75	S. W.	str. br. rain	squally	rain	
3	69	80	W. S. W.	str. br.	rain	rain	
4	68	81	S. W.	rain	rain	rain	
5	70	74	from S. W.	gloomy	gloomy	gloomy	
6	76	78	S. W.	cloudy	cloudy	cloudy	
7	68	69	S. W.	str. br. rain	cloudy	rain	
8	65	70	S.	cloudy	cloudy	cloudy	
9	66	70	S. by E.	fair	fair	fair	
10	70	74	N.	fair	fair	fair	

Days;	Thermometer.		Winds,	Weather.			Remarks.
	Sun rise.	Noon.		Morning.	Noon.	Night.	
Nov. 11	73	75	N. N. E.	fair	fair	fair	
12	75	75	S. S. E.	rain	cloudy	fair	
13	69	71	S.	str. br. clo.	cloudy	cloudy	
14	58	74	S. S. E.	str. br.	squ. rain.	rain	
15	64	70	S.	cloudy	cloudy	cloudy	
16	59	72	S. S. W.	fair	fair	fair	
17	58	62	S. W. N.	fair	fair	fair	
18	60	74	W. S. W.	fair	fair	fair	
19	57	64	S. E.	hv. squ. rain	fair	rain	
20	59	64	S. S. W.	squ. rain	fair	fair	
21	77	80	Calms	fair	fair	fair	
22	64	70	S. W. N.	str. br. rain	heavy squ. and rain		
23	57	60	N. W. W.	heavy squs. thund. lightning, and rain throughout			
24	72	76	S. W. S.	dark gloomy weather, squalls and rain throughout			
25	74	74	W. S. W. S	fair	cloudy	cloudy	
26	76	78	Calms	fair	fair	fair	
27	70	76	variable	fair	squ. rain	fair	
28	69	71	N. W. S. W.	heavy squs. thund. lightning, and rain throughout			

Date			N.E. S.W.				Remarks
Nov. 29	70°	74	N.E. S.W.				heavy squalls with thunder, lightning, and rain, and a heavy shower of hail at 11 A.M.
30	70	72	W. N.W.				heavy squalls and continual rain
Dec. 1	58	59	W. N.W.				heavy gale with severe thunder, lightning, and rain
2	58	76	N.W. S.W.				heavy squalls, thunder, lightning, and rain
3	74	78	W. S.W.	fair	fair	fair	
4	74	76	Calms	fair	fair	fair	
5	74	78	E.N.E.	fair	fair	fair	
6	60	90	Calm N.W.	fair	fair	fair	At 1 P.M. a strong puff of wind from N.W. raised the thermometer from 70° to 90° in a few minutes.
7	77	80	S.W.W.	str. br.	cloudy	cloudy	
8	75	77	S.W.	squally	cloudy	cloudy	
9	69	75	S.W.S.	fair	fair	fair	
10	70	74	S.W.	fair	fair	fair	
11	60	70	S.W.	fair	fair	fair	
12	59	61	S. by E.	fair	fair	fair	
13	61	73	S.S.E.	fair	fair	fair	
14	68	72	S.	fair	fair	fair	
15	70	76	S.S.W.	dark cloudy	cloudy	cloudy	
16	70	75	S.W.	fair	fair	fair	
17	58	59	W.	fair	fair	fair	

N° IV.

(Page 193.)

Observations on the various kinds of Timber
found in New South Wales.

NEW South Wales produces a great variety of
timber trees, to some of which the colonists have
given names descriptive of their qualities, and
others they call by the names of those trees which
they most resemble either in leaf, in fruit, or in
the texture of the wood. Among the former are
the blue, red, and black butted gums, stringy and
iron barks, turpentine and light wood; and
among the latter are the she-oak, mahogany,
cedar, box, honeysuckle, tea-tree, pear-tree,
apple-tree, and fig-tree. These trees shed their
bark annually at the fall of the year, and are
always in foliage, the new leaves forcing off the
old ones.

The blue and red gums are nearly of the same
texture; they are very tough and strong, and in

6   ship-

ship-building are adapted to framing; the best size is from two feet to two and a half, for when larger, the timber is generally unsound in the heart. The blue gum, while standing, is subject to be pierced by very minute worms, which make innumerable holes scarce visible to the naked eye.

Black butted gum and stringy bark differ very little either in quality or appearance; they are much tougher and stronger than English oak, and are particularly adapted to planking. They will also answer for lower masts or lower yards, for beams, or any other purpose where straight timber is required. If intended for spars, they ought to be procured as near the size wanted as possible, for the toughness lies in the outside, and the wood at the heart is generally decayed. Iron bark is not so tough as the two former, but is extremely strong and hard, and runs good from two to four feet; in ship-building it would answer for framing, beams, &c. In New South

Q   Wales,

Wales it is chiefly used in house building and common furniture. Turpentine is a small wood of no service but in flooring houses. Light-wood grows to twenty inches, and from its buoyancy (whence its name), is proper for building small craft and boats.

The oak is distinguished according as it grows either on the hills or swamps; the former runs to between twelve and eighteen inches, and when larger is always shaken in the heart, the grain is short and cross, and the wood is apt to fly and warp; it is used chiefly in cabinet work, particularly vineering. The swamp oak is the same size, and differs from the other in having a more uniform grain, and being consequently much tougher; in ship-building it would answer for scantling. Of both these woods the paling and shingles are made in New South Wales.

Mahogany runs good to three feet, and by its texture can scarcely be known from the mahogany

gany of Jamaica. In ship-building it answers well for framing.

Cedar nearly resembles the mahogany of Honduras in its grain, and might be applied to the same purposes. When growing, it resembles the mountain ash, both in its leaves and berry.

Box (so called from its leaves) is a sound and very tough wood; its size about two feet and a half, and would answer for any purpose of ship-building.

Honeysuckle (named from its leaf) is a soft wood, fitter for joiners' work than ship-building. At Port Jackson its size does not exceed two feet, but at Port Philip it is found good to four feet; its limbs are crooked, and perhaps it might be advantageously used in the upper works of ships, for knees, &c.

The tea-tree has its name from the leaf also, it is small and very curly; as far as I know, it has never been used in building, but from its ap-

pearance,

pearance, while standing, I should think it might answer in small craft and boats.

The pear-tree is so called from its bearing a fruit resembling a pear in shape, but of the hardness of wood; it grows straight, its largest size sixteen inches, and is only fit for joiners' work.

The apple-tree takes its name from the leaf, the limbs are large and crooked, and running from two feet to two and a half, might probably answer for framing and kneeing ships, but has never been tried.

The fig-tree is the banyan tree of the East Indies, well known for its branches striking downwards and taking root; the wood of it is entirely useless.

It may be remarked, that all the large timber trees of New South Wales, except those growing in swamps, are unsound in the hearts : this probably proceeds from insufficiency of moisture,

as

as well as from the continual firing of the grass
in the forests, which must dry up the sap of the
young trees. It also deserves to be noticed, that
several of the gums, iron, and stringy bark,
mahogany and box trees, which were felled at
the first establishment of the colony, are now
perfectly sound and hard, though exposed to the
weather for fifteen years.

From the foot of the Blue Mountains* specimens of three or four kinds of timber, unknown

at

* This is an elevated ridge running in a direction
between the E. N. E. and E. and not more than five
leagues from the banks of the Hawkesbury at Rich-
mond Hill. All beyond this ridge is literally a *terra
incognita*, for though several attempts have been made
to pass them, not one has yet succeeded; but it is probable these failures have proceeded more from want of
proper method, or of common perseverance, than
from any obstacles presented by the mountains themselves, for the highest part of the ridge does not appear to equal the common mountains of Wales and
Ireland. Upon this subject (as well as upon others
of the colonial system) we may apply the remarks of a

Q 3   learned

at Port Jackson, have been brought, which, it is the opinion of shipwrights, would be very valuable in ship-building: one kind in particular cannot be known from the beech.

---

learned writer, " Projects thought desperate in days of ignorance have, in more enlightened times, been brought to a successful issue;" and " individuals have often failed in their attempts for want of public encouragement, and public enterprizes from want of concurrence among individuals."

Weight of a cubic foot of the timber of New South Wales.

Wt. when cut down, Jan. 1804.		Wt. at the present time Aug. 1304.
	lbs.	
Gum, red -	79	
—— blue -	68	
—— black butted	71	
Bark, stringy -	67	
—— Iron -	74	
Mahogany -	66	
She-oak -	65	
Box - -	77	
Tea-tree -	69	

N°

N° V.

Observations respecting the selection of convicts for transportation, and on the means of preserving health on the voyage.

UPON the proper selection of convicts to be transported to a new colony, its improvement must almost totally depend. The advice of Lord Bacon upon this subject is worthy of attention. " The people wherewith you plant," says his Lordship, in his essay " on Plantations," ought to be gardeners, ploughmen, labourers, smiths, carpenters, joiners, fishermen, fowlers, with some few apothecaries, surgeons, cooks, and bakers." How little such a selection is attended to in the transportation of convicts to New South Wales, was sufficiently exempli-

Q 4

fied

fied on board the Calcutta, where, out of three
hundred and seven convicts, there were but eight
carpenters and joiners, three smiths, one gardener,
twenty labouring farmers, two fishermen, nine
taylors, and four stone-masons. The remainder
may be classed under the heads of gentlemen's
servants, hair-dressers, hackney-coachmen, chair-
men, silk-weavers, calico-printers, watch-makers,
lapidaries, merchant's clerks, and *gentlemen*. It
requires no argument to demonstrate the little
use such trades are in an infant colony, where
agriculture is the chief pursuit, and where manual labour is infinitely more necessary than ingenuity. It is true a watch-maker deals in me-
tals as well as the smith, but we doubt whether,
with all his exertions, he could make a hundred
nails in a day. With respect to *gentlemen convicts*, they are worse than useless, for they are
invariably troublesome, as the present government of New South Wales can sufficiently attest.
The education and the manners of such people
will,

will, in most instances, prevent their being employed in manual labour; they will always find ad-
vocates in the feelings of those who hold the
rank which they once held, and this will prevent
their being confounded with the common herd
of convicted felons : but, although by their crimes
they have lost the reality of their original rank,
the shadow of it remains, together with a portion
of the feelings which constituted their former
character ; hence they contemplate their degrada-
tion with impatience bordering on phrenzy ;
they are guilty of indiscretions (particularly in
language) which must create continual disturb-
ance to an administration, where coërcion is the
only engine of government, and where consequently jealousy is continually on the watch to
anticipate insurrection.

The method of selecting the convicts sent out
in the Calcutta might certainly be improved. A
list

list of four hundred convicts was sent to the surgeon of that ship, from which he was to choose
three hundred.   In this selection, he, of course,
regarded merely health and age, for he was to
receive 10l for every convict landed in health in
New South Wales.   Of their characters he could
have no knowledge, and he had no instructions
respecting peculiar trades, in preference to
others.

The dreadful mortality which has, in several
instances, taken place among the convicts on
board transports going to New South Wales,
must proceed chiefly from a want of attention to
cleanliness, both in the persons of the convicts
and the ship herself; for, in every instance where
proper precautions were taken, no such mortality
has taken place.   The convicts, in general, being
equally indolent and careless, as well as unused
to a ship, will in many instances be found so

2   negligent

negligent of themselves, that severity is sometimes necessary to prevent their becoming the
most difgufting objects from vermin and dirt.
In passing through the warm latitudes in particular, the most rigid attention to cleanliness can
alone prevent disease; the following precautions,
if strictly followed, will, as far as it is in the
power of man, prevent the admission of sickness, or effectually check its progress, in the
most crowded ship. When the prison is on the
orlop deck, where the air has but a scanty admission, it should never be wetted, the dirt
should be scraped off every morning, and the
deck afterwards scrubbed with bibles * and dry
sand.

Every part of the prison should be clean, so
that no receptacle for bones or other filth could
be found; and should it be necessary to stow any

* These are blocks of wood a foot long, and six
inches deep and wide.

articles

articles whatever in the prison, the space they occupy ought to be bulkheaded round. Particular care is requisite that no wet cloaths are hung up or left about the prison.

Every convict should be supplied with a hammock*, a very thin mattress, and one blanket; care must be taken that every man hangs his hammock up in his proper birth, else laziness will induce the greater number to spread it on the deck even in the wet; in dry weather the beds should be aired as often as possible, (if every day the better,) and the hammock scrubbed once a month.

If the ship touches at Teneriffe or Madeira, or if not, after she has passed those islands, the

* This was done on board the Glatton and Calcutta, but on board hired transports fixed bed-places are usually erected for the convicts, from which it is probable their bed-things are never removed while they are on board.

beds,

beds, blankets, jackets, stockings, shoes, and
every kind of woollen clothing, should be taken
from the convicts, else, from the total want of
fore-thought, the greater part of them will be
lost, before they again feel the want of them in
the high southern latitudes. The flocks in the
beds should be taken out, and, after being exposed
to the sun, remade; all the woollen-clothing
well-washed (if the ship touches at the islands, in
fresh water, if not, in salt), and afterwards dipped
in lime-water, and dried without wringing. The
fumigations, by means of devils composed of
wetted gun-powder, are perhaps often carried to
too great an excess, and, in fact, this kind of fumigation is liable to many and great objections, particularly in cold or wet weather, when it is most
commonly practised; the cold air, rushing into
the fumigated apartments when opened, immediately condenses the vapour that remains, and leaves
a degree of dampness that must be unwholesome.

In

In wet weather it is impossible to let a sufficient quantity of air into the apartment after fumigation, without, at the same time, admitting a proportionate quantity of moisture; hence the people often return to it before the vapour is evaporated, and inhale a considerable quantity, which must affect the lungs. In all weathers, fires of sea-coal (for charcoal is liable to the same objections as fumigations with gun-powder) will be found infinitely more effectual in clearing the prisons of foul air, than any kind of fumigation. As to fumigation by acids, it is usually performed on so small a scale, that I cannot conceive it productive of any advantages, if any such are inherent in it.

In passing through the warm latitudes, I would strongly recommend, that the convicts be *obliged* to bathe, at least, twice a week. This might be so regulated as to give but little trouble, a certain proportion bathing every day, and if performed

formed under the superintendence of a medical man, no danger could arise from it. In short, it will be found, that wholesome diet, sufficient exercise, and proper attention to cleanliness, are the most effectual preventives of disease on long voyages. The first, the Government of England supplies with a liberality peculiar to itself; but the two latter must be left to the care of the person to whom the charge of so many of his fellow-creatures is entrusted.

THE END.

Printed by Strahan and Preston,
New-Street Square, London.

For EU product safety concerns, contact us at Calle de José Abascal, 56–1°,
28003 Madrid, Spain or eugpsr@cambridge.org.

 www.ingramcontent.com/pod-product-compliance
Ingram Content Group UK Ltd.
Pitfield, Milton Keynes, MK11 3LW, UK
UKHW010341140625
459647UK00010B/739